Quarterly Essay

T0357925

1   DRAGON'S TAIL
The Lucky Country after the China Boom
Andrew Charlton

75   CORRESPONDENCE
Mary Crock, Michael Bachelard, Neil James, David Corlett,
Andrew Hamilton, Paul Toohey

101   Contributors

Quarterly Essay is published four times a year by Black Inc., an imprint of Schwartz Media Pty Ltd. Publisher: Morry Schwartz.

ISBN 978-1-86395-656-7 ISSN 1832-0953

Subscriptions – 1 year (4 issues): $59 within Australia incl. GST. Outside Australia $89. 2 years (8 issues): $105 within Australia incl. GST. Outside Australia $165.

Payment may be made by Mastercard or Visa, or by cheque made out to Schwartz Media. Payment includes postage and handling.

To subscribe, fill out and post the subscription card or form inside this issue, or subscribe online:

www.quarterlyessay.com
subscribe@blackincbooks.com
Phone: 61 3 9486 0288

Correspondence should be addressed to:

The Editor, Quarterly Essay
37–39 Langridge Street
Collingwood VIC 3066 Australia
Phone: 61 3 9486 0288 / Fax: 61 3 9486 0244
Email: quarterlyessay@blackincbooks.com

Editor: Chris Feik. Management: Sophy Williams, Caitlin Yates. Publicity: Elisabeth Young. Design: Guy Mirabella. Assistant Editor/Production Coordinator: Nikola Lusk. Typesetting: Duncan Blachford.

Printed by Griffin Press, Australia. The paper used to produce this book comes from wood grown in sustainable forests.

DRAGON'S TAIL | The Lucky Country after the China Boom

Andrew Charlton

In the sunlit residence of the Australian Embassy in Beijing, on a mild and clear afternoon in August 2008, the ambassador's staff were preparing a banquet for the prime minister. The mini-tornado that precedes every prime-ministerial event was swirling around them: security guards checking cars, advisers finalising briefing notes, minders arriving early to jostle their boss's name-card closer to the centre of the table, and chefs preparing the West Australian rock lobsters flown in for the occasion.

The Beijing embassy was designed to weave together Chinese and Australian architectural traditions. Viewed from the street, the chunky grey walls capture the *hutong* character of the ancient capital's networked alleys and courtyard residences. But once visitors pass through the entrance, they are drawn into a grassy interior quadrangle that evokes the relaxed openness of suburban Australia. The lawn hosts frequent summer barbeques and the embassy bar offers a reliable year-round supply of Australian beer and good cheer.

If embassy buildings are architecture as diplomacy, a physical expression of bilateral relations, then Australia's Beijing mission sends a mixed message. Though the thick concrete edifice captures the spirit of old Beijing, it also betrays a sense of guarded isolation. Constructed in an era of diplomatic tension – after the Tiananmen tragedy, but before the economic renaissance under Jiang Zemin – the embassy is built for security. Diplomats live in an autonomous compound topped with spikes of gleaming metal around a fortified perimeter. If the building exhibits a distinctive "Australianness," it is that of a wary tourist decked out in sunglasses and cargo shorts, cash and passport tucked away in a concealed money pouch.

As the prime minister arrived at the banquet, the guests were already seated and trading staccato pleasantries across the table through translators. Australia's mining titans lined up on one side of the table: BHP's Marius Kloppers, Rio Tinto's Tom Albanese and Fortescue's Andrew Forrest. Facing them were China's metal moguls, including Xu Lejiang of Baosteel, Huang Tianwen of Sinosteel and Xiao Yaqing of Chinalco.

Collectively, the men in this room were responsible for the rivers of iron-rich red dirt that flow inexorably north across the ocean from Australia's desolate ancient landscapes to China's teeming new megalopolises. Australia's resources have been China's bounty and salvation, raising cities from the ground, lifting tens of millions of people out of grinding poverty and allowing the government to build a new system of ports, highways, airports, railroads, bridges, buildings and tunnels. As one of the world's largest exporters of both iron ore and coal, Australia supplies China's life force, the juice in its machine.

One year before the meeting, this symbiosis had been ruptured. As China's hungry steel mills masticated ever-larger quantities of iron ore, Australia's miners seized a once-in-a-generation opportunity for profit. Abandoning the convention that had set global iron-ore prices for more than thirty years, BHP and Rio demanded a huge one-off 85 per cent price increase.

The Chinese were furious. They feared that if costs for steel producers rose, this would in turn push up costs for a wide range of companies, from car-makers to construction firms, and damage China's entire steel-centred economy. The Chinese media accused the Australian miners of acting like a "cartel."

The pall of this conflict hung in the room. But the Chinese guests hadn't come to the banquet today to reopen the wound. They were focused on the future. Twenty years ago, Deng Xiaoping, the architect of modern China, had cautioned his people to build their global power patiently: "Hide your brightness, bide your time." Now China's time had come. China had leaped from emerging economy to global superpower. But to realise its ambitions, it needed a reliable supply of fuel for its economic engine. Access to resources was no longer a commercial matter – it was a strategic imperative.

*

According to the version of history popular among the Chinese elite, their country is emerging from a "century of humiliation." For a hundred years China was degraded, bullied and torn apart by foreign imperialists. The British demanded punitive concessions after their victory in the Opium Wars; the French seized control of territories that now make up northern Vietnam; and Macau was lost to Portugal in the Treaty of Peking. The deepest wounds were inflicted by the Japanese during the decades that stretched from the annexure of Taiwan to the rape of Nanking and the ferocious policy of *Sanko Sakusen* ("kill all, loot all, burn all") that led to the deaths of millions of Chinese civilians towards the end of World War II. Remembrance of this period serves as a focal point for Chinese nationalism. The Chinese Communist Party uses the sense of victimisation to bolster support, crediting itself with pulling China out of the century of humiliation and deriving its own legitimacy from a national narrative of loss and redemption known as *fuxing* or "rejuvenation."

If the Chinese needed a galvanising symbol of *fuxing* – and they did – they could not have asked for a better one than hosting the Olympic Games. On the day of the banquet, the streets around the Australian Embassy were full of athletes and spectators from around the world. International visitors could not help but be impressed by the new Norman Foster–created Capital Airport and the Olympic Park with its dramatic Herzog and de Meuron–designed "bird's nest" stadium. Gone were the grimy Soviet-style apartments, ramshackle courtyard houses and defoliated streets, replaced now by broad boulevards, skyscrapers and luxury flats. The Games were testament to China's rejuvenation. "The glow of the Games," wrote the *China Daily*, "should have dispelled any lingering bitterness from the humiliating defeats China suffered at the hands of imperialist aggressors in the past century."

Just as China's athletes had their role in *fuxing*, so did the businessmen at the banquet. The next step in their nation's progress was to exert influence abroad – what the Chinese call the policy of "going out." One of the first priorities of "going out" is to secure the raw materials the economy needs. China's domestic reserves can meet demand for fewer than half of forty-five strategic minerals. By 2020 it will have a sufficient supply of only six. "Based on its current industrialisation trajectory, China has no choice but to move upstream in the resource industry," wrote the Chinese financial newspaper *Caijing*. "At stake is the long-term sustainability of an economy with an immense appetite for resource inputs." Acquiring such assets gives China security of supply and some influence over prices. To put the purpose of "going out" bluntly: as China's economy grows, it doesn't just want to trade Australian resources, it wants to own them.

The Chinese guests at the banquet were the front line in this advance. Xiao Yaqing, president of the massive metals conglomerate Chinalco, had spearheaded the campaign. Months earlier he had launched a daring midnight raid on Rio Tinto, splashing $11 billion to buy a 10 per cent stake in the company. It was the largest foreign investment ever undertaken by a Chinese company.

Xiao's raid on Rio Tinto wasn't a business decision; it was geopolitical conflict with commercial weaponry. In taking a stake in Rio Tinto, he was acting for the Chinese government as it sought to strengthen its position in the global iron-ore market. For more than a year, there had been talk of BHP and Rio Tinto combining forces to create an iron-ore behemoth. Pushed by its new CEO, Marius Kloppers, BHP planned to gobble up Rio and thereby gain unprecedented power over the supply of raw materials to the world. The prospect of a combined BHP and Rio struck fear into the hearts of Chinese officials, who worried the merged entity would force their steel industry to pay even higher prices.

A member of the Central Committee of the Communist Party as well as a captain of industry, Xiao Yaqing personified China's blurry line between politics and business. He was the perfect instrument to thwart BHP's ambitions. Xiao's raid came on 1 February 2008, just four days before Kloppers was expected to put forward his bid. "Chinalco's purchase has successfully prevented the merger of Rio Tinto and BHP," boasted the government-controlled *Global Times*, "broken the monopoly of multinational giants, and protected our nation's core interests." Following the raid, Xiao was hailed as "a national hero for promoting overseas acquisitions."

Xiao was flanked at the banquet by other pioneers of China's "going out" strategy. Huang Tianwen had recently launched a hostile $1.2-billion takeover of the Australian iron-ore producer Midwest Corporation and was now building a stake in a second iron-ore company, Murchison Metals, with a view to building a huge hub in central Western Australia. Also at the table was Wang Tianpu, president of the Chinese oil giant Sinopec, which had spent $600 million to buy Australia's Puffin and Talbot oilfields in the Timor Sea. Beside him, Lou Jiwei, China's former vice minister of finance, had been tasked with the establishment of the China Investment Corporation, a fund to invest the Chinese government's vast wealth abroad. Australian resources companies were at the top of Lou's shopping list.

All in all, there had been twenty-six Chinese proposals to acquire Australian resources companies in the previous year. The sudden deluge of applications was generating concern in Australia. "The Australian government would never be allowed to buy a mine in China," declared the

Nationals senator Barnaby Joyce in a television ad. "So why would we allow the Chinese government to buy and control a key strategic asset in our country?" Spooked by the publicity, the Australian government began to back-pedal, announcing it would take steps to ensure that Chinese government–backed "investment and sales decisions are driven by market forces rather than external strategic or political considerations." That statement, and its implied accusation, ricocheted around Beijing. The Chinese guests had come to the banquet today to hear the Australian prime minister clarify his position on their investment proposals.

Kevin Rudd bounded into the room and took his place in the centre of the table. From what the Chinese knew of him, Rudd was the perfect prime minister to help them. He was their Manchurian Candidate – the man who could bring Australia into China's orbit, navigating around the political barriers to a closer economic relationship.

Rudd sat down at the table and greeted the guests warmly in fluent Mandarin. Not understanding a word, one of the Australian businessmen joked, sotto voce: "Is he on our side or theirs?"

*

In Chinese philosophy, natural contrasts – such as light and dark, high and low, hot and cold, fire and water, life and death – are interconnected. It is impossible to talk about one without reference to the other because they are bound together as parts of a whole. There cannot be a flower without seeds, nor seeds without a flower: one reaches its zenith, then dies back to make way for the other. There cannot be a society with only men or only women: the interaction of the two gives birth to further generations. No country is more intertwined with China's economic rise than Australia. Now joined together, we will rise and fall as one. We are yin and yang.

As microhistory, the embassy banquet was an allegory for the kindred journey of the two nations. For three decades Australia and China had come together in a confluence of history and geography, in which China's vast demand for raw materials was perfectly complemented by Australia's extraordinary natural endowment. Despite that history, this essay argues that China's economic relationship with Australia is still poorly understood.

Australians have a tendency to look at our national issues through an insular domestic lens. Our national debates are frequently partisan and parochial. For example, if you are on the right, you know that the budget is now in deficit because Labor wasted money; if you are on the left, you know that a deficit was necessary to save hundreds of thousands of jobs. On the right, you know that Australian manufacturing jobs are disappearing because we are uncompetitive with our Asian neighbours; on the left, it's because Australian industry doesn't receive the same subsidies that those of other countries enjoy. On the left, you would argue that the global financial crisis was caused by greed and lax regulation of financial markets; on the right, you might point the finger at excessive government debt. If you are on the right, you know that Australia pulled through the financial crisis because John Howard left Australia with a strong surplus; on the left, it was because of Kevin Rudd's economic stimulus. On the right, you know that productivity growth is low because powerful unions disrupt workplace efficiency; on the left, it is because Australia hasn't invested sufficiently in skills and infrastructure.

These positions are easily digestible and often self-serving. But they are all either wholly wrong or drastically incomplete because they overlook the events beyond our borders that have shaped us. In this essay we will discover that much of Australia's current situation is due to finding ourselves in the jaws of a once-in-a-century economic circumstance. China's industrialisation is perhaps the most significant economic event since the Industrial Revolution that transformed Britain in the eighteenth century and laid the framework for the modern world. And China's industrialisation has occurred 100 times more quickly and on a scale 1000 times larger than Britain's Industrial Revolution.

Few nations have been affected more by China's transformation than Australia. China helps explain why Australia has experienced two decades of unprecedented prosperity, why our house prices have soared, why we survived the financial crisis. And China also helps explain many of our challenges, why so many of our manufacturing businesses are struggling, why the dollar is so volatile, why our competitiveness is slipping, why the budget is in the red.

The economic state of Australia today can only be explained in the wider context of our region; and, most importantly, only by thinking in that wider context can we create a path to future prosperity.

The *Economist* recently devoted its front cover to an image of the Australian continent coloured in gold. The title read "The Next Golden State." Inside, the magazine devoted sixteen pages to what has been variously described as the world's "miracle economy" and the "wonder Down Under."

Magazines can be prone to hyperbole, but the remarkable story of Australia's economic success requires no exaggeration. Over the last twenty years, Australia's economic growth has been no less than one-third faster than the United States', twice as fast as Europe's, and three times faster than Japan's. Australia's growth rate – the most reliable barometer of our progress towards a better, or at least richer, future – is faster than that of any other comparable economy, and ours has been the longest period of sustained prosperity of any developed country in the modern era.

This performance is all the more remarkable because it was so unexpected. The 1980s were tough sledding for Australia. Our economy struggled through booms and busts; we were written off as "the poor white trash of Asia" by Singapore's legendary prime minister Lee Kwan Yew; our own treasurer, Paul Keating, wondered aloud whether we would become a "banana republic"; and our Reserve Bank governor conceded that "little hope was held for our economic future." As the 1980s closed, a million families lost their livelihoods to a painful recession. At the end of that sober decade, our best days seemed behind us.

Then, against all expectations, the tide began to rise. Slowly at first, then at pace, we caught a wave of prosperity that swelled into a tsunami. Since then our rate of progress has been so fast that it has outpaced even our ambitions. In the early 1990s Australian optimists aspired to be in the "top half" of OECD nations. We achieved that before the decade was out. In the new millennium, the government put forward the goal of reaching the top ten nations by income per capita by 2015. It was achieved within two years. Our success has surprised none more than ourselves.

All this has brought Australia to something of a *jour de gloire*. By 2013,

Australians had become the seventh-richest people in the world. And most of the nations richer than us are small states: Luxembourg, Qatar, Norway and Switzerland. We are the richest of the major economies in the world.

*

A few years ago I received a call from a former colleague, Laura Alfaro, now a professor of economics at Harvard University. She was ringing to ask for help with a research project. "What's the topic?" I enquired.

Her response came out of the blue: "Australia."

I found myself chewing the air for a moment. A medley of competing responses came to mind. Why would Laura, a Costa Rican economist at Harvard University, be interested in Australia?

"I really want to understand how Australia did it," she said. "How you became one of the richest countries in the world?"

I groped for a response, then, after a pause, replied: "Australia is the Lucky Country."

I was embarrassed before the words left my lips. An indolent reflex? Possibly. A transparent cliché? Certainly. Horne coined that tired old phrase fifty years ago as a reproach to a nation he scorned. But time has since worn away his meaning, inverting it into a strange affirmation.

This question – why Australia of all countries became so rich and stayed so rich over such a long period of time – is perhaps the most important question facing our nation. The fact that our response tends to be so glib speaks to a national complacency that should be very worrying. Most of us take prosperity for granted and relax with a Micawberish faith that, no matter what the world throws at us, "something will turn up."

Part of the problem is that explaining national prosperity is hard. There are many factors that contribute to it. To understand how Australia became rich, consider the graph below. If there were only one graph of Australia's economy, this would be it: each bar represents Australia's economic growth rate in each year since 1820. This chart is the story of our prosperity. But be warned: this graph is not a "clear," in the sense that it has a simple message that jumps off the page. In fact, you might look at this graph for hours and not come away with much more than a headache. Prosperity is complex!

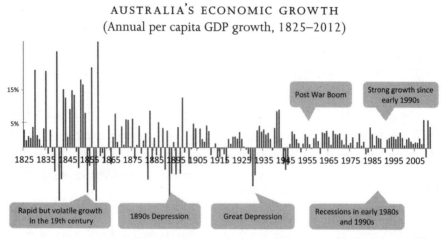

AUSTRALIA'S ECONOMIC GROWTH
(Annual per capita GDP growth, 1825–2012)

Source: Historical Statistics of the World Economy, Angus Maddison, 2008; World Bank WDI 2013.

A few things can be made out from the graph. The first is that most of the bars are positive. This general upward trend – what we refer to as economic "progress" – is the statistical image of growth. Australia's average income per capita has risen, on average, by 2.1 per cent a year, measured in constant international dollars. That might not sound like much, but over nearly 200 years it means incomes have risen more than sixty-fold.

The second thing to notice is that the rate of growth is not constant: sometimes the graph's bars are up, sometimes they are down. If you look closely, you will see some of the landmarks of economic history: the deep falls in growth in the late nineteenth century from 1890 to 1900, during the depression of the 1930s and during the world wars. You can see smaller falls – recessions – in the early 1980s and 1990s.

These seismic global events make the graph very hard to interpret. Overwhelmed by depressions, wars, booms and recessions, it is hard to get much purchase on the real story of Australia's success. To understand Australia's performance – independent of what is going on around the world – we need to take out the impact of these global economic events. One way to do that is to measure Australia's performance relative to other nations. That way we can strip out much of the volatility caused by events that affected the whole world. In the graph below I've used a unique historical dataset produced by Angus Maddison, who pieced together gross domestic product (GDP) data for a large number of nations over several centuries. Using this data, I've compared Australia's income per capita with that of other countries.

When we look at Australia's economic performance in this way, the scales fall from our eyes. The long history of our economy can be summed up in a single sentence: Australia had a very good nineteenth century, a poor twentieth century and a stellar start to the twenty-first century.

AUSTRALIA'S GLOBAL RANK
(Australia's position in the world's richest countries measured by GDP per capita)

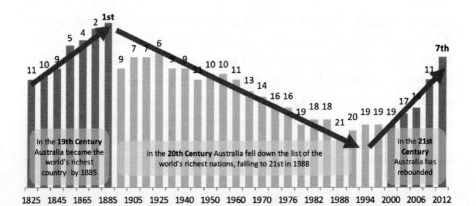

Source: Author's calculations from: Historical Statistics of the World Economy, Angus Maddison, 2008; World Bank WDI 2013.

Our success in the early nineteenth century was due to agriculture. Governor Hunter despatched two ships to Cape Town in 1796 to bring back supplies for the New South Wales colony. An enterprising soldier, John Macarthur, asked the travellers to return with some sheep. By a happy coincidence the King of Spain had recently given some of the finest pure merino sheep from the jealously guarded Escurial flocks to the Dutch government and these had found their way to the Cape colony. These merino sheep were bred into the core stock of the colony and proved remarkably well suited to the production of high-quality wool in Australia.

Farming in the colony picked up steam following the discovery of large expanses of natural grassland for livestock in eastern Australia. Australian farmers were successful because they were remarkably productive. In fact, woolgrowers in particular quickly achieved efficiency levels above the rest of the world because Australian graziers had a number of important advantages: they faced very low land costs (squatters having in most cases paid nothing for their tracts); there was no need to build barns (the temperate Australian climate meant that sheep could be outdoors all year round); and there was no requirement to stockpile hay or hand-feed through the winter (Australian sheep grazed on natural grassland rather than cultivated fields). All this meant that colonial farmers were among the most efficient in the world. By 1850 more than half the wool in the clothing and blankets woven in British textile mills was being shorn from Australian sheep, which by then numbered 16 million.

Just sixty years after white settlement, Australia had become the seventh-richest country on the planet by grafting European farming onto the southern continent. Up until that point, Australia's wealth was sourced from surface resources – forests and fisheries, pelts, whaling, grazing, cropping and timber – but in the next year Australians discovered that the real treasure was below their feet.

In 1851 Edward Hargraves reported the discovery of gold at Ophir in western New South Wales. Hargraves, an avuncular Englishman on the make, had just returned from the Californian diggings, where he witnessed the transformative mania of a gold rush engulfing a colonial society. What Hargraves did not know is that the rush he would start in Australia would last for more than forty years; would spread around the continent, with major discoveries in New South Wales, Victoria, Tasmania, Queensland and Western Australia; would create some of the most cosmopolitan cities on earth; and would make Australians the richest people the world had known.

News of the rush inspired wanderlust in depression-affected Britain, with one paper reporting that "the country, from the mountain ranges to an indefinite extent in the interior, is one enormous goldfield." Immigrants leaving Britain in 1852 bought more tickets to Melbourne than to any other city in the world. Thousands arrived every day, packing lodging houses, hotels and shantytowns on the city's edge. The rush to board ships at Liverpool and Plymouth was large enough to reverse the slump in English ship-building. Reaching Melbourne, one vessel had to drop anchor twenty kilometres out to sea to prevent its crew jumping ship to join the rush. By the end of the decade, one person in every fifty in the British Isles had sailed south on the promise of the great southern land.

The long decline in the centre of the chart makes clear that Australia didn't have a very good twentieth century. Starting in 1890, Australia commenced a long and steady deterioration in its position in the league of wealthy nations. Over the next 100 years Australia declined from top to twenty-first in the world, as measured by per capita GDP.

Why did the nation's fortunes fall so far? At the end of the nineteenth century Australia faced the classic problem of a resources-based economy in which commodity prices drop away. After a century of success, these falling prices convinced Australians that our resources would be the cause of long-term national decline. There was a general lament that we had too small a manufacturing base and were too dependent on "commodities" produced by the rural and resources sector. This pessimism motivated the creation of the policy framework that has come to be known as the "Australian Settlement" – a semi-tacit compact dating from the time of federation, designed to prop up Australia's industrial sector. Manufacturing businesses were propped up by tariffs and subsidies, manufacturing workers' jobs were protected from foreign competition by the restrictive "White Australia" immigration policy, and manufacturing incomes were guaranteed by centralised wage-setting.

Australia's relative prosperity began to fall as its share of manufacturing grew. The problem was that, by contrast with resources and agriculture, Australia did not have the same advantages in the production of many goods. Our farms and mines were among the world's most productive, but our factories and saleyards were not. As manufacturing became a larger part of the economy, its relatively low productivity dragged on our growth, leading us to be overtaken first by more efficient industrial powers, including the United States and a host of European countries, and later in the century by Japan, Singapore and other dynamic Asian countries to our north. Of course, Australia did have periods of prosperity in the twentieth century – there was a short boom in the 1920s and a longer boom following World War II – but these were not unique to Australia and did not lift us up the global scoreboard.

The problem, as former prime minister Paul Keating said, was that:

> the Australian economy was locked up and uncompetitive and the dollar was too high in value so it was killing miners and farmers particularly … The internationally competitive ones, the ones that dug up coal, iron ore, lead and zinc, were barely competitive because wages were too high and the exchange rate was too high.

In the last two decades Australia has reversed much of the century-long decline in our national standing. First, Australia's terms of trade – the ratio of export prices to import prices – bottomed out in 1986 and have risen since. It has not been an even rise, but each subsequent trough has been at a higher level than its predecessor. Second, the Australian Settlement which entrenched our manufacturing weakness was dismantled as governments of the left and the right carried out the reforms that have given Australia one of the most open economies in the world. In the 1980s the incoming Labor government led by Bob Hawke floated the Australian dollar, liberalised the financial system, put an end to import quotas and slashed tariffs. Paul Keating and John Howard continued the reforms. By 2003 much of the Australian Settlement had been pulled apart. The effective rate of protection in manufacturing had fallen from about 35 per cent in the 1970s to 5 per cent. Corporate and income taxes had both been reduced. Foreign banks had been allowed to enter. Many government-owned firms had been privatised. The telecommunications, energy and transport industries had been deregulated. And the labour market was more flexible, with centralised wage-fixing replaced by enterprise bargaining. These reforms prised the four big prices in our economy out of the grip of government, allowing the price of capital, the price of labour, the price of our currency and the price of imported goods to be set by the market. The combination of these reforms and the improvement in commodity prices sparked a boom that arrested the decline in our national fortunes and made us once again one of the richest countries in the world.

*

What do these three periods tell us about the source of our prosperity? Australia is a large land mass with a small population and abundant natural resources.

Our mineral wealth is globally significant. Australia has the largest demonstrated lodes of uranium, nickel, lead, zinc and brown coal of any country in the world; the second-largest demonstrated reserves of bauxite, copper and silver; and the fourth-largest reserves of iron ore. In all, Australia has a staggering 19 per cent of the world's total known mineral wealth. Given that we have 0.3 per cent of the world's population, this means that every Australian has more than fifty times our fair share of minerals, based on an equal allocation across the world. Beyond minerals, we have large assets of timber-yielding forest, farmland, coast and wilderness, as well as energy. Adding up all our natural resources, Australia is the second-richest nation on the planet by natural wealth per capita outside the oil-producing economies.

Primary industries make up a relatively small share of total employment, but they account for a huge share of exports and a significant proportion of foreign investment. They also have a disproportionate impact on a wide array of related industries. That is not to say that there aren't many other important sectors in Australia's economy. Or that there aren't many other business success stories. But our primary industries help take us from being a middling country on the world's stage to a living-standards superpower.

Australia's fortunes depend on the value of our resources on world markets. When the world price of our commodity exports is high, we are richer. When the world price falls, as it did for much of the twentieth century, Australia is poorer. As we will see later in this essay, resources by themselves do not guarantee economic success (in fact, for many countries the opposite is true), but for Australians resources have been at the heart of our prosperity.

THE SECRET OF CHINA'S SUCCESS

If you want a picture of the transformation that has occurred in China over the last twenty years (and to know why Australia is going through the biggest commodity boom since the gold rushes), look at the jaw-dropping difference between the two photographs below.

These are photographs of the world's largest city, Shanghai, taken from the same vantage point twenty-three years apart – in 1990 and 2013.

In the centre of the photographs is the jutting peninsula of Lujiazui, now known as the Pudong New Area. In the earlier photograph, the region is mainly shanty homes, with some warehouses and wharves near the shore. Today, Lujiazui is Shanghai's answer to Manhattan. The transformation began in the early 1990s, when the Chinese government decided to set up a Special Economic Zone, intended to become the new financial hub of modern China. In 1991 construction began on the striking Oriental Pearl Radio and Television Tower, visible on the left side of the more recent photograph. At 468 metres high, the Pearl Tower was the tallest structure in China until it was surpassed in 2007 by the Shanghai World Financial Center (also in that photograph and recognisable by its distinctive trapezoidal void). With 100 floors and reaching 492 metres, the super-tall skyscraper was at one point the highest roof in the world. At the time of writing, the World Financial Center has been surpassed by the building to its right, the new 125-storey Shanghai Tower, which when completed in late 2014 will be China's tallest building at 632 metres high.

The dramatic transformation of Lujiazui stands in contrast to the western side of the Huangpu River, visible in the lower part of the photographs, where the old financial district known as the Bund is largely unchanged. The Bund was a British settlement conceded in the 1842 Treaty of Nanking following China's military defeat in the First Opium War. Under British influence, Shanghai flourished as a cosmopolitan financial centre and was hailed in the 1920s as the "Paris of the East." In photographs you can see some of the magnificent Beaux-Arts-style commercial buildings constructed in the late nineteenth century by British, French and American trading companies. For China, the Bund is a painful reminder of the past, a remnant of the century of humiliation. This was a time, in the words of nationalist president Sun Yat-sen, of "economic oppression by the foreign powers" that dissolved China into "a heap of loose sand."

The Chinese are not always subtle. The modern skyscrapers of Lujiazui are a vivid expression of new financial power – a physical manifestation of fuxing. They sit directly across from, and now dominate, the vestiges of Western colonialism in the historic Bund.

For the Chinese, these two photographs represent a profound change in their national circumstances. Since Deng Xiaoping began instituting market reforms in the late 1970s, China has been the fastest-growing economy in the world, with annual GDP growth averaging, until recently, above 10 per cent for the last three decades. This growth has increased the size of its economy tenfold and created as many new jobs each year for twenty years as the total number of people employed in Australia.

China's spectacular rate of economic growth over three decades is unique in modern history. Only Japan, Taiwan, South Korea and Singapore have achieved similar sustained growth, but none of these has matched China's scale. In fact, the Chinese economic miracle may have done more to improve the state of humanity than any other event in our lifetimes. Since 1981, 600 million people in China have emerged from poverty. This is certainly one of the great economic achievements – and human achievements – of the last century.

*

"Let China sleep," Napoleon Bonaparte warned, "for when she awakes, she will shake the world." That awakening is now upon us. Understanding China's economic growth is important for the world. China's economic ascendancy underwrites its growing global power, perhaps the defining force of the twenty-first century. Nobody knows how China's ascent will play out, because there is no precedent: the world's most populous nation has never been its richest, and there has never been a superpower from outside the Western-oriented world order. We do not know whether rising China will support trade and mutuality with the West, or whether it will launch an epic battle over the rules and leadership of the international system. Will East and West peacefully share global power, or will China follow Mao's monomaniacal maxim that "political power grows out of the barrel of a gun"? Understanding China's growth trajectory is essential to grappling with these global questions. Understanding China's growth is also profoundly important for Australia as we craft a national strategy to seize the opportunities it affords and avoid the risks it poses for us.

The first thing to say about China's economic-growth strategy is that it is not new. China's policies are merely the latest (and largest) application of the well-known economic model used to drive rapid growth in many countries throughout the twentieth century. As we will see, all of the countries that have implemented this growth model have done so in somewhat different ways, but three universal features are essential to its success.

First, the country must have a strong government. All successful applications of the "investment-led" growth strategy have been implemented by authoritarian governments, often autocracies or one-party states. A strong state is necessary because the strategy requires massive government intervention in the economy – often against the interests of a minority (or even a majority) of the population.

Second, the model requires the government to confiscate resources from its people. The growth model works by suppressing consumption, which means forcing people to accept lower living standards in the short term in return for faster economic growth. As we will see, there are many policies that explicitly or implicitly confiscate resources, including high taxation, suppressed wages growth, currency depreciation, powerful state-owned businesses and financial-market intervention. All applications of the investment-led growth strategy have used some combination of these policies.

Third, the model requires the government to use resources confiscated from its people to fund rapid growth of investments (and often exports). Again, there are a range of policies available to achieve this, but most countries use some combination of state subsidies, low wages, subsidised borrowing and powerful state-owned enterprises.

Together, these three elements help ensure that a poor country will grow quickly. To see how the model works, consider a very simple example. Imagine a poor country with a lot of unemployed people. Now imagine the following scenario: a new authoritarian government comes to power (element 1), imposes a big tax on all employed people (element 2) and uses the proceeds of the tax to pay a state-owned company to build a new road (element 3). What happens to our imaginary country? Well, each worker's consumption falls because the new tax has reduced people's disposable income. And investment rises because the tax proceeds are used to invest in new road infrastructure. What happens to economic growth? Well, more people are employed in the construction of the road, so unemployment falls and the size of the economy increases. This example is cartoonishly simple, but it does capture the essence of the strategy used to deliver rapid growth many times throughout the twentieth century.

Germany used this model to deliver rapid growth in the lead-up to World War II. In June 1933, the "Reinhardt Program" was introduced to spur investment in waterways, railroads and autobahns. In 1936 Hitler issued the "Four-Year Plan Memorandum," which increased state intervention in the economy, siphoned off resources from the population through rationing of food, clothing, metal and wood, and massively boosted investment in infrastructure and munitions. The plan had a military objective, but the formula for growth was familiar: resources were transferred from consumption to investment, growth was rapid, unemployment fell quickly and Germany emerged strongly from the Great Depression.

Beginning in 1928, the Soviet Union implemented another version of the same model through a series of Five-Year Plans aiming to transform a mainly agrarian society into a major industrial power by the 1950s. Soviet economic planners divided the economy into "Group A" industries, which included all investment (industrial products, factory equipment, infrastructure, etc.), and "Group B" industries, which included all consumer goods (food, clothing and shoes, appliances, etc.). From the early days of the Stalin era, Group A industries took priority in economic planning and allocation of resources. The Soviet government suppressed consumption by ensuring workers were paid as little as possible. The people were told that they should make sacrifices today in order to realise a magnificent utopian future. This reached an apotheosis during Stalin's collectivisation of agriculture, as peasants had their last stocks of grain seized from them in order for the government to export it abroad and use the profits to fund industrial expansion. From its impoverished state in 1919, the Soviet economy grew strongly, industrialising rapidly, developing successful heavy industries, and even putting the first man-made satellite into orbit in 1957. Nikita Khrushchev, the Soviet leader, felt emboldened to declare, "The time is not far distant when we shall catch up with and surpass the United States." The rapid economic growth of the Soviet Union became a major political issue in America, with John F. Kennedy moved to declare, "We stand today on the edge of a new frontier; are we willing to match the Russian sacrifice of the present for the future?"

In the last quarter of the twentieth century, Japan, Taiwan, Korea and Singapore all followed a similar strategy, which led many economists to call it the "Asian growth model" or "state-led development" path. The Asian countries had a greater focus on exports, but the three key ingredients at the centre of the model were the same – as were the model's consequences for growth, which are mixed over the long term.

There are three sectors of an economy: consumption, investment and net exports (exports minus imports). This means that everything produced is either consumed (for example, food, goods and services are consumed by the private and public sector) or invested for the future (for example, used to construct houses, factories and roads) or exported (shipped to foreigners in exchange for imports). In a balanced, modern economy all these components grow at roughly the same rate over the long run. This provides some stability, ensuring that living standards (which are related to consumption) grow at the same rate as the economy, and that exports and imports are roughly in balance. In countries pursuing rapid growth, these three sectors do not grow together. The government intervenes to accelerate the growth of investment above the growth of consumption and, usually, the growth of exports above the growth of imports. Over time the investment and export sectors become more and more dominant, which, as we will see, creates underlying and ultimately unsustainable imbalances. Note that all the countries named above were successful in using this strategy to drive rapid growth for a period, but almost all experienced significant and, in some cases, devastating challenges as a result.

*

China's economy is the latest and largest application of this growth model. It clearly has the first ingredient: a strong authoritarian government. The Chinese Communist Party is the world's largest and most powerful one-party regime. Economic planning is central to its rule. The Chinese government exerts enormous control over the economy through its massive bureaucracy and highly regulated markets. Large parts of the economy are organised through a huge apparatus of state-owned enterprises, which account for more than a third of business activity. China explicitly directs the national economy through its Five-Year Plans – colossal documents, methodically listing challenges, initiatives and targets that touch every corner of Chinese social and economic life, from health care and alternative energy to school sports programs.

China also has the second ingredient: policies that move resources from its people to the investment and export sectors. One of the most prominent mechanisms is China's management of its currency. Most mature economies allow their currency to "float," such that the value of a currency – the exchange rate – is determined by market forces. In China the exchange rate is managed by the government, which has, to varying degrees over the last two decades, acted to reduce the value of its currency. Many scholars reckon that the yuan was 20–25 per cent undervalued for most of the last decade.

Artificially suppressing the exchange rate is effectively a consumption tax on ordinary Chinese people. To see why, notice that if the yuan is devalued by 25 per cent, then the cost of everything Chinese people buy from abroad increases by 25 per cent. Ordinary Chinese people buy lots of imported goods, including food and energy. A lower yuan means they must pay more for all such imports, leaving them less money for other purchases. In short, when the government lowers the value of the yuan, it reduces the living standards of its people.

If the Chinese people lose (at least in the short term), then who benefits? Chinese exporters receive a huge benefit because their products are cheaper on world markets. If the price of steel is, say, $750 per tonne, then after a 25 per cent depreciation in the Chinese currency the Chinese exporter is able to offer steel for just over $550 and get the same value in yuan. This means that the Chinese steel company is more competitive and able to capture a larger share of the international steel market. The impact of this currency depreciation is the same as offering a 25 per cent subsidy on all Chinese exports and imposing a 25 per cent tariff on all foreign imports of steel. This is a tremendous benefit to exporting companies. It enables a big increase in steel exports, a big increase in steel production and a big increase in employment in the steel industry. China's currency is a key element of its growth model. It is a state intervention designed to expand the economy by transferring resources from consumers to the export sector.

As well as using its currency to redistribute resources, the Chinese government also holds down wages. For many years, it kept wages low by facilitating the movement of workers from rural areas to the cities fast enough to ensure that factories never had to offer large wage rises to get the workers they needed.

Since 1978 China has experienced the largest internal migration in human history. More than 200 million people have moved from rural areas into cities to find work. Coastal cities like Shenzhen, just over the border from Hong Kong, have ballooned, growing from a small town in 1978 to a sprawling city of more than 12 million people today. "It's a new world for us in the city," said Tian Wei, who left his wheat farm in the province of Hebei to take a job as a factory nightwatchman. "All my life

I've worked with my hands in the fields." Now Tian and millions of other rural folk have found new lives for themselves in the city.

The knowledge that millions of countryside workers were looking for jobs in the cities enabled Chinese employers to keep the real wages of low-skilled workers almost flat during the 1980s and 1990s. "For years, businesses have simply assumed that China has an unlimited supply of young people who can be had for modest wages and replaced at will," says the economist Arthur Kroeber. Most employers take the view that if you are not happy with your 1000-yuan wage, you can leave – there are plenty more workers willing to accept it.

The Chinese government controls the supply of labour to the cities through a system called the hukou. Each citizen is registered in the area in which they were born. This registration entitles them to receive social services, including health care, housing, employment and education, in their specific area. The hukou means many families are separated for years. Huang Daofeng and her four children stayed behind in their farming village while her husband worked in a copper refinery in the city of Tongling in Anhui province 400 kilometres away. "All I wanted at that time was to move to the city," said Ms Huang, now seventy-one years old. "What mattered was for the family to be together." At opposite ends of the province, she and her husband got to see each other once a year for eighteen years.

The hukou system helps the government manage the labour market and keep wages low. It ensures that workers arrive in the cities rapidly enough to supply the export sector with workers, but slowly enough to prevent political dissent fermenting in pools of urban unemployment. If too many people arrive in the city at once, Chinese leaders fear the advent of the squalid shantytowns that pockmark other developing cities such as Manila, Mumbai and Rio de Janeiro. Slums can be cauldrons of social unrest and political instability. The hukou helps to ensure that housing and infrastructure development keeps pace with urban growth.

The Chinese government also keeps a lid on wages by circumscribing trade-union activity. The government sanctions one trade union, the

ACFTU, which has more than 200 million members. All other industrial organisations are banned. Until recently, the ACFTU focused on employees of state-owned enterprises, where its main function is to maintain discipline and prevent interruptions to production. Tim Pringle, the author of Trade Unions in China, says Chinese labour organisations are "primarily an instrument for controlling the working class," rather than representing them. When workers at the Nanhai Honda car plant in China's Pearl River Delta walked off the job against the advice of the ACFTU in 2010, one striking worker told the New York Times, "The trade union is not representing our views; we want our own union that will represent us." Striking workers had to fend off a gang of heavies sent by the ACFTU to prevent them picketing.

The result of these policies is that Chinese wages have lagged behind economic growth. In a modern economy, wages should grow in line with the rest of the economy, but in China wages growth has been much slower than overall economic growth.

To say that wages growth has been low does not mean that Chinese people in aggregate are not better off under the investment-led growth model. Individual wages have grown much more slowly than overall economic growth, and workers' share of total income has been falling as more profit is gobbled up by companies, the government and the political elite. But millions of additional people were lifted out of unemployment and subsistence agriculture, so in aggregate Chinese people are better off. Just as with the currency depreciation, low wages growth represents an implicit tax on workers which subsidises their employers. It is another means of boosting the competitiveness of businesses to fuel rapid growth in exports, investments and jobs.

A third major policy the Chinese government has used to support its investment-led growth model is financial-market regulation. In particular, the Chinese government sets the interest rates that people earn on their savings. In February 2002, deposit rates were set at just 0.72 per cent and held there for six years. This meant that Chinese households with a large part of their wealth in savings were earning a very low rate of interest. Even worse, the rate of inflation in China was very high, reaching 8 per cent in 2008. This meant that, accounting for inflation, the real interest rate was actually negative 7.28 per cent – putting money in the bank eroded the real value of savings.

By keeping interest rates low, the Chinese government was reducing the income of families with savings – effectively imposing a huge hidden tax. If Chinese people get such a raw deal from their savings deposits, why don't they put their money elsewhere? If such rates were kept artificially low in Australia or the United States, people would respond by transferring their wealth into shares or other investments, or by sending it overseas. But in China it is difficult to take money out of the country, and stock markets are undeveloped, highly risky and prone to insider trading. Many Chinese invest in real estate as an alternative to bank deposits, but the property market has high transaction costs and limited liquidity, so it is not suitable for people who need to gain access to their savings at short notice. "What makes China's form of financial repression unique," says economist Michael Pettis, "is the limited investment alternatives for household savings, a situation reinforced by capital controls." Many ordinary people have no alternative but to accept very low deposit rates on their savings.

Who benefits from China's low interest rates on savings? Again, the beneficiary is the investment sector. Low deposit rates translate into low interest rates for borrowers raising money to finance projects, especially property developers, construction firms and manufacturers building new factories.

These three policies – low currency, low wages, low interest rates – are central to China's growth model. Each of these policies supports Chinese industry to invest and export. Each policy serves to expropriate income from Chinese families, reducing their income in real terms. These policies are Robin Hood in reverse – they take from the poor to give to the rich, with the underlying rationale that the rich corporations will use the subsidies to create more jobs for new workers.

*

It might sound unfair to take resources from people to subsidise business, but it is hard to argue with the success of the growth model. China has achieved double-digit growth rates over the previous three decades. Over time, the whole country, including its poorest people, has become better off as a result.

This is the trade-off at the heart of the Chinese social contract. The Chinese Communist Party is authoritarian and undemocratic. It denies the Chinese people basic democratic rights and it limits freedoms of speech, association and religion. It confiscates their resources through a range of hidden taxes on their income. Yet the Communist Party enjoys support among the Chinese people. The core of this political bargain is the trade-off between short-term freedom and long-term growth. The Chinese government implicitly says to the Chinese people that they must surrender political rights and living standards in the short term in return for greater benefits in the future.

In the next chapters we will look at the other side of the coin. China's growth model has driven vast domestic economic transformation, but its effects don't stop at the border. China's growth has had an enormous effect on the rest of the world. When China's currency goes down, another currency must be going up. When China's trade balance is in high surplus, another country must be running a trade deficit. When China is exporting its excess savings abroad, another country must be importing capital. In this chapter we have seen that China has pursued growth by introducing massive imbalances and distortions into its economy. We will now consider the impact of these distortions on other countries, and show that much of what we have observed around the world, and particularly in Australia, has had its roots in China's astonishing transformation.

I'd been waiting for my meal for forty minutes at the Boardwalk Brasserie in Cairns when Darren, the proprietor for many years, came over to explain. "Sorry," he said. "Bit understaffed. The cook left yesterday." Darren had given his chef a 20 per cent pay rise six months ago. Last week he had asked for another 25 per cent. "I told him I couldn't afford the first rise." Darren's chef had been offered a job working in the mines. He preferred to stay in Cairns, where his young family were settled in school, but as the mines expanded, "Every month he had another offer – more money every time." Darren had no option but to pay more. Yet chefs still left to work in the mine kitchens, waiters left to become cleaning contractors, taxi drivers left to drive trucks. "The mines are like a war ... all the good young men around here get sucked away."

Darren had once taken Monday and Tuesday nights off, with a manager covering the shifts. Two years ago, as the cost of staff kept rising, he decided to close the restaurant on those nights. "It was the wages, but it wasn't just the wages," he said. Business slowed down as well. "First the Asian tourists slowed right down." When Darren opened his restaurant in 2000, the Australian dollar was 50 cents to the US dollar. Australia was a cheap place for people to come, and Cairns was a short flight from some of Asia's fastest-growing cities. As the dollar rose, more than doubling to $1.10 by 2011, Cairns became a more expensive place to visit and the tourism industry suffered. Qantas stopped flying its route from Singapore to Cairns in 2007, and stopped bringing Japanese tourists directly to Cairns in 2009. "The dollar was a cruncher. All the foreign tourists stayed away because Australia was too expensive. Then all the people from Sydney and Melbourne started holidaying in Bali and Thailand because it was so cheap."

Cairns illustrates the contradictory impact of China on Australia. On the one hand we have become very rich, but on the other we have lost competitiveness. This is the paradox of Australia's prosperity. "In recent years, this region has lost much of its 'punch' in economic terms," acknowledges

Cairns's mayor, Bob Manning. "We have lost industries and many of our larger companies who were significant employers. Our economic base is now far too narrowly focused, and business confidence has suffered greatly." Cairns is a microcosm of the Australian economy and the conflicting forces buffeting us.

*

China's growth formula made Australia very rich. Large parts of China (and of other developing countries following the same path) have been construction sites for more than a decade. Remorseless developers scour ancient villages, clearing away the past without regret, replacing the dust and grime of traditional life with the shiny steel and glass skylines of Western cities.

Australians are thousands of kilometres from Asia's glitzy new metropolises, but we are providing much of the physical backbone to the narrative of fuxing. Steel is the critical building material in the construction of skyscrapers, transport infrastructure, residential towers, factories, electronic appliances, household goods and the many other manufactured products that Asia exports to the world.

When the first of the two photographs of Shanghai in the previous chapter was taken, in 1990, China used 50 million tons of steel every year – about half the quantity used in the United States. By the time the skyscrapers had been built, China's construction and manufacturing industries were using around 700 million tons of steel – nearly six times that used in the United States.

China's steel boom has been Australia's good fortune. China's own resources are not sufficient to meet demand, forcing it to look to resources-rich neighbours for commodity inputs. The two key inputs for steelmaking are iron ore and coking coal. Australia has an extraordinary abundance of both.

One guest at the Beijing embassy banquet in 2008 personifies the impact of China's industrialisation on Australia. Andrew Forrest is as Aussie as a sandfly bite. His great-great-uncle John Forrest was the first premier of Western Australia and, before that, a prodigious explorer whose lengthy expeditions across unknown desolation helped to map the arid state. Andrew Forrest, too, pushed through the desert, but rather than driving horses and camels he laid parallel steel rails to move the ferrous earth from Cloudbreak to Chinese ships at Port Hedland.

When Forrest acquired his Pilbara ore tenements, few believed he could make them pay. The deposits were bought cheaply because they were thought to be "stranded" – that is, the cost of getting the ore to the port was deemed to be greater than the value of the asset in the ground. Forrest was able to buy the tenements for a song.

What Forrest saw was a mega-trend – a game-changing spike in demand for steel that would transform the economics of iron ore. It would turn stranded ore bodies into buried treasure. In 1990 China consumed just 4 per cent of total globally traded iron ore, but by 2010 this had risen to a staggering 61 per cent. When Forrest bought the tenements, the price of iron ore was around US$20 per tonne and the price of Forrest's Fortescue Metals Group stock was just three cents. By the time he had built a railway and developed the mine, iron-ore prices were over $100 per tonne, Fortescue's share price had rocketed to $7.50 and Andrew Forrest was Australia's richest man.

Forrest's is one of Australia's great business success stories. It's also a perfect symbol of the impact of China on Australia's mining sector. The rush to build new mines and expand existing pits set off a construction boom that washed through the whole economy. The high incomes from the mining sector spilled beyond the resources regions, and every Australian felt richer as a result of the rising value of their equity wealth, held directly or through superannuation accounts, and the largesse of a government flush with windfall revenues.

China's growth model has benefited Australia in another important way. Australia exports vast quantities of natural resources to China, but it also imports vast quantities of goods from China: $44 billion worth each year. That is $2000 for every Australian. China's export success has made it the workshop of the world. Today China produces two-thirds of the world's shoes, socks and toys; half of the world's DVD players, digital cameras and microwave ovens; one-third of its desktop computers and T-shirts; a quarter of its mobile telephones, TV sets and radios – and so on. China is Australia's largest source of imports, accounting for a fifth of all goods brought into the country. Australians buy so many Chinese goods in department stores and clothing shops because they offer better value than the alternatives – and are cheaper than ever before. This makes us richer, because the cheaper our clothes and electronic goods, the more money we have to spend on other things. Imports from China make Australians richer.

This is only helped by China's growth model that subsidises exports – making them even cheaper for Australians to buy. If the Chinese currency is 25 per cent undervalued, then every Australian is saving hundreds of dollars every year on the Chinese goods they buy, all thanks to the Chinese government.

The combined impact of exports and imports on Australia's wealth is measured by our terms of trade. These improve when either the price of Australia's exports rises, or the price of what we import falls. Over the last decade our terms of trade rose to the highest level since the gold rushes of the mid-nineteenth century.

To put Australia's terms of trade wealth in simple terms: ten years ago, a shipload of iron ore exported to China was worth about the same as 2200 flat-screen televisions imported from China. Today the same shipload of iron ore is worth 22,000 flat-screen televisions! Iron ore has become more expensive as the global demand outstrips global supply, and televisions have become cheaper as China ships them at lower and lower cost. This illustrates how China's rise has improved our standard of living: as a result of changing prices, Australia is now exchanging the things we export for ten times more of the goods we import.

*

Another way China's growth model has benefited Australia is through financial markets. As we have seen, the Chinese government regulates the supply of its currency. For much of the last decade, China's currency was kept artificially low and this helped China run a large trade surplus with the rest of the world. One consequence of the trade surplus was more people seeking to buy the yuan (for example, foreigners needing yuan to pay for Chinese exports) than people seeking to sell the yuan (for example, Chinese people seeking to pay for foreign imports). And since the government was controlling the market, it had to be selling more yuan for foreign money than it was buying. The point is that in the context of a controlled exchange rate and a trade surplus, the government is forced to accumulate foreign money. And this is precisely what happened in China on a grand scale. As a result of its interventions in currency markets, the People's Bank of China has amassed a staggering US$3 trillion in foreign exchange.

China's build-up of foreign currency assets has had tectonic implications for the rest of the world. The Chinese government invested this money abroad – for example, it lent $1.3 trillion to the US government, becoming the largest foreign holder of US government debt. And it lent trillions more to governments and companies around the world. This huge torrent of money flowing from China (and other trade-surplus countries, including Germany and the oil exporters) into the United States, Australia and many other countries produced a worldwide surplus of investable funds, which economists dubbed the "global savings glut." These surplus funds pushed down the cost of debt – that is, interest rates fell as finance became more readily available. In the United States and Europe, interest rates fell to below 2 per cent in the early 2000s, and in Japan they fell to below 1 per cent. Suddenly credit was cheap. In Britain, where records go back a long way, interest rates on long-term government debt fell to the lowest levels in nearly 300 years.

What happened to all this cheap debt? It helped to finance boom conditions across the Western world. Much of the ready credit found its way into real estate, fuelling soaring prices in America and Europe. Over the five years from 2001 to 2006, house prices increased dramatically, nearly doubling in cities as disparate as Las Vegas, Reykjavík, Dublin and Madrid. Some of the money found its way into global stock markets, driving extraordinary gains between 2002 and 2007 around the world, including on the US stock market – up nearly 80 per cent – and the British FTSE – up 70 per cent. In Australia the global savings glut helped to finance a boom that pushed up house prices and caused the Australian All Ordinaries index to more than double.

With interest rates low, investors found they were getting only meagre returns on their funds. These low returns encouraged bankers and other financial professions to try to help investors increase their yields by taking on more risk. The bankers created financial products such as "subprime" loans, complex derivatives, collateralised debt obligations and other exotic instruments. These "dodgy assets" peddled by "greedy bankers" have worn much of the blame for the financial crisis of 2008. Certainly, unscrupulous bankers and slack regulators should not be let off the hook for their part in the crisis, but they were riders on a wave. The elemental force was the tidal flow of money pouring out of the savings-glut countries.

Ultimately, the crash came when the interlocking bubbles in real estate, stocks and financial assets burst. House prices tumbled, stock markets collapsed and many of the complex financial assets turned out to be worthless. Around the world, the human consequences of the crisis were devastating. Countless families lost their homes and life savings, and the United Nations estimates that more than 50 million people were put out of work as a result of the global recession that followed the crisis.

When the global financial crisis hit, the Chinese premier, Wen Jiabao, was quick to point the finger at the United States. In early 2009, just months after the crisis began, Wen told the World Economic Forum that the cause of the crisis was the "excessive expansion of financial institutions in a blind pursuit of profit" in Western countries and the failure of Western governments to supervise their banks properly, "which allowed the risks of financial derivatives to build and spread." He went on to blame the capitalist culture of the United States and Europe for an "unsustainable model of development characterised by prolonged low savings and high consumption." Unfortunately, that explanation is both self-serving and incomplete. For one thing, it flatters the power of the bankers, who were irresponsible bit-players in a much larger drama. Second, what Wen didn't acknowledge was China's role. In fact China (along with other surplus countries) played a central role in creating the underlying imbalances that led to the crisis. China's growth model created the glut of cheap goods that resulted in a massive Chinese trade surplus and a massive US trade deficit; China's huge glut of savings was then lent back to the United States to finance its credit boom and help fuel its property bubble. The world is a system and what happens in one country might originate in another. China was on the other end of the seesaw when the US economy crashed.

Australia fared better than most countries during the crisis. Many factors helped us, but ironically, China's own response to the crisis was important. When the impact of the crisis was first felt in China, the government responded swiftly with a huge infrastructure program and a directive to state-owned enterprises to continue to invest. The resulting construction led to a rapid recovery in metal prices that sustained the Australian resources boom.

*

In 2013 the World Bank published its World Development Indicators, which showed that Australia had risen to be the seventh-richest nation in the world, our highest position in more than a hundred years. In the same year the World Economic Forum published its ranking of the competitiveness of nations, The Global Competitiveness Report, which soberly announced that "this edition marks the first time that Australia exits the top twenty." We had tumbled to twenty-first position.

These global competitiveness rankings can be subjective, and they are far from the only way to measure efficiency and productivity, but it is striking that Australia should be falling in the competitiveness tables at the same time as we are rising to the top of the income league. How is this possible? How can our economy be leading the world in income growth but falling behind in competitiveness? To answer this question, let's go back to Cairns.

Blessed with the Great Barrier Reef and extraordinary rainforests, Cairns should be experiencing a tourism boom. Yet the number of international tourists arriving in Far North Queensland has dropped by 25 per cent over the past few years. "This isn't because the reef is suddenly less beautiful, or that the region's tourist operators are doing something wrong," says Mark Ogge of the Australia Institute. "It is because international tourists are faced with the high Australian dollar, which has been driven up by the mining boom. The simple truth is that the boom has made Far North Queensland a far more expensive tourist destination, which is costing local jobs and businesses." At the same time as foreign tourism dwindles, domestic holiday-makers are scarce. "Rising incomes make overseas holidays more attractive, and the rising Australian dollar makes them more affordable. The number of Australians heading overseas over the recent holiday period was about a third higher than just four summers ago."

It's not just the tourism industry in Cairns that is struggling – so too are all the businesses that operate internationally, including manufacturing firms that compete with ever-cheaper imports. And even businesses that aren't subject to direct international competition are suffering from higher wages and other costs. The fate of Darren's business is a prime example of this "lost competitiveness." First, it lost competitiveness because costs went up when Darren had to pay his staff more to compete with the salaries being offered on the mines. Second, the mining boom pushed up the Australian dollar, causing Cairns to lose competitiveness against other holiday destinations. Third, and most worryingly, there has been a long-term impact. As the profitability of the industry has fallen, so has investment in new facilities. There haven't been many new hotel developments in Cairns, and many of the tourist attractions are looking faded. "The buzz has gone," says Darren. "Even if the dollar falls, I wonder whether the tourists will want to come back to Cairns."

The same forces affecting Cairns are rippling across Australia. In December 2013, General Motors finally announced that it would cease making cars in Australia, ending sixty years of Holden production here. A few months later Ford advised that it would shut down the Ford Australia engine and vehicle plants in October 2016, and Toyota said it too would quit Australian manufacturing in 2017. The Mitsubishi Motors Australia plant in Adelaide had already closed in February 2008. Holden's managing director, Mike Devereux, said, "We are witnessing a huge shift in … the wider economy of Australia," brought about by the "sustained strength of the Aussie dollar against almost all major trading currencies, the relatively high cost of production, and the relatively small scale of the local domestic market." Once Holden exported to seventeen countries; now Australia imports vehicles from no fewer than twenty-seven countries. Australian manufacture of cars rose to a maximum of almost half a million in the 1970s and still exceeded 400,000 in 2004. As the currency rose and Australians felt richer, they purchased fewer domestic cars and more imported vehicles. By 2009 just 210,000 Australian-made cars were sold. The Victorian premier, Denis Napthine, says automotive manufacturing is important for Australia. "It is important in terms of jobs, but it's also vital for manufacturing capacity, for skills capacity, for the future of these areas in our economy."

Cars, tourism and many other non-resources industries are examples of the paradox of Australia's prosperity. China's boom has made us richer than we have been for a century, but it has also drained the competitiveness from many parts of our economy. This leaves us in a vulnerable state. We have put a lot of eggs in one basket and our economy is highly leveraged to international circumstances. The question is: are the good times over?

Looking into the middle distance across the wide Avenue des Champs Élysées, you are immersed in the nuance and ambiance of the City of Lights. The boulevard stretching out in front of you is lined with apartment blocks, whose pitched mansard roofs punctuated by dormer windows are the recognisable signature of Haussmannian architecture.

In one direction, you have a clear view of the renaissance Fountain des Quatre-Parties-du-Monde, with its striking circle of eight galloping horses appearing to splash through the water. In the centre of the fountain, on a pedestal above the spray, stands Jean-Baptiste Carpeaux's neoclassical bronze masterpiece: four standing nudes – representing Europe, Asia, Africa and America – twisting their outstretched limbs as they turn the armillary above their heads. Carpeaux's message is that the four peoples of the world hold a fragile, mutual purchase on the peace of the world.

Turning to the south, you catch a glimpse of perhaps the world's most stirring architectural landmark and the highest expression of the modern metropolis. The Eiffel Tower is an enduring icon of Paris and its contribution to the world. Erected on the centenary of the French Revolution, it was designed by Gustave Eiffel as an expression of gratitude for the "century of industry and science" that followed the rebirth of the nation at the Bastille.

In this city, the charm and beauty of the Belle Époque surround you. The only problem is … you are not in Paris. In fact, you are more than 8000 kilometres from France. You can see a few clues around you: bamboo trellises support newly planted trees, the skies are heavy with a thin mist that bears the scent of pollution rather than precipitation, and the city is a little too new – it has the unmistakable gleam of a freshly forged banknote.

This is not Haussmann's city. It's a replica Paris called Tianducheng in the Chinese province of Hangzhou. Like most Chinese counterfeits, Tianducheng is a good copy of the original. It even has a horse-drawn buggy that clip-clops across the cobblestones each day to a yellow church at the top of a hill, where, for a fee, a "priest" in white-collared robes will perform wedding ceremonies at an altar hung with a cross.

Tianducheng is one of many replica cities in mainland China. There is a Thames Town near Shanghai that boasts Victorian terraces, cobbled streets, a gothic cathedral and corner shops on the theme of a classic British market town. Hangzhou has a replica Venice, complete with grand townhouses overlooking a network of canals and stone bridges navigated by gondoliers. The town square has every feature of Saint Mark's except for the pigeons and the flooding.

The pinnacle of Chinese "duplitecture" is the Window of the World complex near Shenzhen. A 108-metre replica of the Eiffel Tower shares a skyline with the Pyramids of Giza, the Leaning Tower of Pisa, the Taj Mahal and, flatteringly, the Sydney Harbour Bridge.

Tianducheng, Thames Town and Venice Water Town aren't theme parks. They are home to thousands of people. Bianca Bosker, author of a book on China's architectural mimicry, says living in a replica city brings no stigma of imitation: "It can be a sign of technological achievement and cultural achievement and it's not inferior." Howard French, a former *New York Times* Shanghai bureau chief, says this architectural movement "is a statement of having arrived, of being rich and successful. It says, '[China] can pick and choose whatever we want, including owning a piece of the West. In fact, we're so rich we can own the West without even having to go there.'"

Construction at Tianducheng began around 2007. It was originally planned as a city for around 100,000 inhabitants. Despite China's love of all things French, the development hasn't been successful for the developers. Only 2000 people have moved in. On the Champs-Élysées, almost every shop is empty. "Some shops did open," says one of the few residents, "but there wasn't much business to sustain them." Wu Xixing, a local woman, says her business might have to close if more people don't arrive.

More people might move in, but for now Tianducheng is a ghost city. And it's not the only one. In 2009 astonishing reports emerged of Kangbashi, a massive uninhabited new city near Ordos in the province of Inner Mongolia. Brand-new office blocks, shopping centres, houses and apartments capable of supporting nearly half a million people stand empty. Weeds are beginning to sprout in luxury villa developments that have no residents. A multi-million-dollar contemporary art museum is completely bare. A government official said, "For a time the cranes kept building more homes in Kangbashi despite blocks of towering new apartments sitting empty and highways that were silent during rush hour. But now even the cranes have stopped and workers have no employment during winter." In 2005 the local Ordos government, cheered on by aggressive developers, had borrowed billions of dollars from state-run banks to build a Chinese version of Dubai — a city rising out of the desert. A local resident,

Yang Zhouluo, said, "The locals all loaned their money and all money has been invested in property. Now nobody can sell apartments and the money is all gone." Others are more optimistic. Zhang Ting borrowed money to buy his apartment. "I know people say it's an empty city, but I don't find any inconveniences living by myself," said Zhang. "It's a new town, let's give it some time."

There are reports of as many as a dozen Chinese ghost towns just like Kangbashi. And on a smaller scale, there are thousands of empty apartment buildings, vacant malls, under-utilised airports and unnecessary roads. In 2003 local government officials in China's Guangdong province, spurred on by billionaire businessman Hu Guirong, planned the world's largest mall. The New South China Mall can accommodate more than 2350 stores and (of course) has seven zones modelled on international cities, which contain a 25-metre replica of the Arc de Triomphe in the Paris zone and a two-kilometre canal with gondolas in the Venice zone. Since the opening in 2005, almost every store has remained vacant.

Tianducheng, Kangbashi and the New South China Mall are extreme examples of a construction boom the likes of which the world has never seen.

*

The investment-led growth model has been used to lift economic growth around the world, from the Soviet Five-Year Plans to the Japanese post-war boom. In the early years, the model produces productive investment that lifts the economy: new factories produce high-quality consumer goods for export to foreign markets; new roads and ports lower the cost of transport of these goods; new apartment towers house workers in the booming export sector; new dams and power stations provide clean water and electricity to burgeoning metropolises. These are productive assets that will deliver strong economic returns and repay the banks and other financiers that loaned the money for construction. Moreover, the growth of investment causes employment to surge as workers move from the countryside to work in more productive urban factories. As growth and employment boom, the investment-led model seems like a no-brainer, so why not let it continue forever?

Unfortunately, it cannot be sustained. The short-term success of the model always convinces observers that the country has found "the secret" to rapid growth, but it never lasts. The model works by distorting the economy, and these distortions bring the model undone.

Two glitches inherent in the investment-led growth strategy ultimately derail the economy. The first is that the distortions introduced to promote excessive investment inevitably lead to poor decisions. Michael Pettis explains that countries "start by powering the economy with investment by the state to build manufacturing capacity and infrastructure. However, the gap between what the country has and what it needs closes quickly, and then it is difficult to recognise what isn't needed." All the subsidies distort investment decisions, leading companies to engage in increasingly marginal or risky projects that would never happen if the companies faced the real costs of capital.

A good example is Brazil in the 1960s and 1970s. In that period Brazil experienced the so-called *Milagre Econômico* ("Economic Miracle"), a time of unprecedented economic growth. When the military grabbed power in the mid-1960s, they installed a young economist, Antônio Delfim Netto, as finance minister. Delfim Netto vowed to turn the poor country into an industrial power and set about guiding Brazil into "important industries" such as steel, oil, heavy construction and mining. Delfim Netto ignored the needs of the population, diverting (often borrowed) resources into Pharaonic infrastructure projects: a multi-billion-dollar new railroad; a subway system in Rio; massive hydroelectric and nuclear plants producing power capacity well beyond current demand. Initially, Delfim Netto's plan was a spectacular success: Brazil recorded six years of real growth averaging 10 per cent a year and the nation entered the era of *Patriotadas* as three football World Cup victories swept Brazilians into a generalised patriotic euphoria. A few years later the miracle expired in a haze of debt and inflation. Excessive investment resulted in unused industrial capacity and Brazil became the world's biggest debtor.

Japan is another country that succeeded in implementing the investment-led growth strategy but subsequently fell into a lost decade of very low growth. In the 1980s, the Japanese stock market was soaring, Japanese companies were expanding across the globe, and "Japan Inc." was the envy of the world. Japan was the first Asian country to challenge the long dominance of the West, and many economists predicted that it would soon overtake the United States as the world's largest economy. Few of the Western management gurus who venerated the "Japanese model" foresaw that only a few years later the Japanese landscape would be dotted with empty office buildings and unused factory space. In 1989 the economy caved in: beginning with a stock-market crash and a real-estate slump, Japan slipped into an economic stagnation that lasted two decades. Looking back, the government admitted that "many of Japan's once-vaunted economic practices are now nothing more than obstacles to future economic development."

As we saw, at the peak of Soviet power in the 1960s, many Western scholars were seduced by its apparent economic strength: America was flooded with heroic photographs of muscular steelworkers and adventurous cosmonauts, and reports of new dams, rockets, factories and satellites. It wasn't all propaganda – the powerful central government was able to rapidly industrialise the Soviet Union. But the investment-led strategy delivered short-term growth which covered over a morass of imbalances and distortions that would lead to collapse a few decades later. Underneath the massive increase in infrastructure and industrial capacity, the productivity of the economy was eroding. The Soviet economy lacked the free-market incentives to get the most out of the investments, to adopt new technologies and improve efficiency. By the 1980s the Soviet people were suffering acute shortages of basic household goods, food rationing and long lines in stores.

Every growth "miracle," whether it be the United States in the 1920s, Germany in the 1930s, the Soviet Union from the late 1940s to the early

1960s, Brazil from the late 1950s to the late 1970s, Japan in the 1980s or Dubai in the 1990s, ends with excessive investment and the discovery that much of the new construction had been a speculative bubble turbo-charged by government distortions. The common thread is a short-term burst of investment-led growth that concealed, and sometimes exacerbated, the underlying weaknesses in each economy.

*

Is China's investment boom headed for a bust? The first thing to say is that China's investment bubble is bigger than anything the world has ever seen. The chart below shows investment as a share of GDP. In most countries investment is around 20 per cent of GDP — which means that most countries choose to consume four-fifths of their production and invest one-fifth for the future. China invests more than double that: a staggering 50 per cent of GDP is directed into new factories, roads, ports, housing and other assets. That means the Chinese people only consume one dollar from every two they earn. This is not only the highest rate of investment in the world, it's higher than that of other countries when going through similarly rapid industrial development — higher than Japan's in the 1960s and Taiwan's in the 1970s, when they were pursuing similar investment-led strategies. More concerning is that the peak of the investment cycle in Japan and Taiwan coincided with the beginning of a big economic slow-down.

Many optimistic observers rationalise China's massive investment binge. They point out that China's road, rail and port infrastructure is still well behind the transport networks in the West and needs further investment. Or they claim that China's urbanisation trend has decades left to run, requiring millions more apartments and hundreds of new airports and subway systems. Far from having too much investment, optimists claim China has a lot more investing to do. The problem with these arguments — which were used, wrongly, to justify every investment-led growth strategy in the twentieth century — is that they assume infrastructure is equally

CHINA'S INVESTMENT AS A SHARE OF GDP

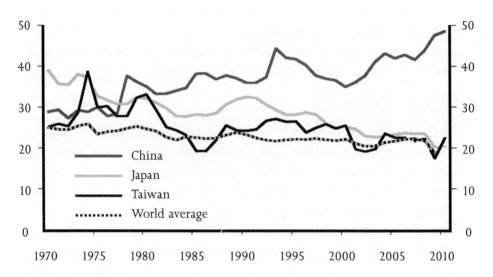

Source: Capital Economics

valuable everywhere in the world. But it isn't. For example, imagine a new subway system is built in an American city to enable the local population to get to work more quickly. American workers are highly productive, their time is valuable and their high wages can more than cover the fares that will fund the subway. Now imagine a similarly sized city in China, where worker productivity is typically just one-fifth of that in America. Because Chinese workers are so much less productive, their wages are much lower and there is a much lower economic return for getting them to work faster. Chinese productivity is much lower than American productivity and justifies a lower level of investment. In fact, spending billions on a subway in China may result in a very large debt for the construction firm or the government. Too much infrastructure means too many bad debts that will undermine China's banks and hurt the economy. Pettis says, "Poorer countries with lower levels of worker productivity are less able, not more able, to absorb very high levels of investment."

Of course, the other problem with the argument is that just because a country may have a general need for more infrastructure, it is still possible to build poor-quality infrastructure. In fact, in the presence of financial and institutional distortions, misallocation of capital is almost inevitable. In the *Times Literary Supplement*, Rosemary Righter described "tens of millions of houses and apartments as well as Ozymandian public buildings and factory estates – and what hits the eye is how much of it all stands empty. Across China, uninhabited concrete blocks scab the land."

The problem of overinvestment ultimately ends in a debt crisis. Poorly conceived investment projects are financed by billions of dollars of debt but do not generate much economic return – the owners of Tianducheng and Kangbashi are not receiving any income from the empty apartment buildings to help them repay their construction costs. In a modern economy, the investors would quickly go out of business, but in China the iron triangle of governments, banks and property developers conspires to keep the investment going. Governments ensure the banks have access to cheap finance by suppressing interest rates on household deposits, banks hide the bad debts by lending even more money to the developers, and developers keep the economy growing by launching ever-larger projects.

With the complicity of governments and state-owned banks, wasteful investment can continue until the whole financial system chokes on bad debt. With their capital locked up in existing projects that are not generating real returns, the only way banks can finance the next round of big projects is by lending more to the developers, some of which they will use to repay old debt and some to start the next construction. "More and more of that new credit is now eaten up paying imaginary returns on the growing pile of bad debt," says Patrick Chovanec of Silvercrest Asset Management. China's banks have been able to afford to take on bad loans because they are generously funded by the deposit system and backed by the government, "but losses are still losses. And in a closed financial system, you can socialise losses, you can spread those losses around, you can brush them under the rug," Chovanec says. "But losses are losses, and somebody bears it and it drags down the economy."

*

Geraldine Doogue brought her interview for ABC's Radio National to a crescendo:

> Dr Shi, your own story, just before I let you go, is so incredible. Born into a farming community, I think that you were given up for adoption, is that correct? And you were raised by adoptive parents, you excelled at school, you then came to Australia, got a job with Dr Martin Green from UNSW, as well as flipping hamburgers in this North Shore café … And here you are now, possibly the richest man in China.

Shi Zhengrong's life is a rags-to-riches story for the twenty-first century. Shi and his twin brother were born to a farming family in the Chinese province of Jiangsu in 1963. Being the younger twin born to parents impoverished by the great famine, Shi was given up for adoption. Arriving in Australia in 1988, he worked at the University of New South Wales, completing a PhD and finding a job at a small Australian energy research company, Pacific Solar.

Fast-forward to 2006 and Shi had moved back to China and was now CEO of Suntech, the world's largest solar panel–maker and the first Chinese company to be listed on the New York Stock Exchange. Shi was named one of *Time* magazine's Heroes of the Environment. In 2007 he was the richest person in mainland China.

Shi's success produced much hand-wringing back in Australia. The then Opposition leader, Kim Beazley, announced that Australia had lost an opportunity to keep Suntech in Australia. Shi's defection, it seemed, symbolised everything that was wrong with Australian manufacturing. It's not right that "China's richest man grows rich off Australian [intellectual property]," Beazley announced. Australia had missed a trick.

Shi agreed. Asked by SBS's *Dateline* why he had decided to leave Australia, the newly minted billionaire blamed the caution of Australian investors and the lack of support from Australian governments: "I can tell you at that time if there were investors in Australia who can really see what is to happen to this industry, or to especially this technology, [and who] can fund the technology in Australia, I guess Pacific Solar would have stayed in Australia."

Shi is right that his business received much more support in China than he could have hoped for in Australia. In 2000, the government of Wuxi city was eager to establish a solar industry. Officials offered Shi subsidies and grants to bring his company to China. "Suntech is a seed sown by the Communist Party committee of the Wuxi government," Shi reflected in a speech in 2011 to open his glittering new headquarters in the city. To the envy of the world, Suntech seemed one more example of China's unstoppable industrial juggernaut, dominating yet another manufacturing sector by flooding the world with cheap products.

But Shi's success didn't last. Last year Suntech filed for bankruptcy. From a market value of $16 billion at its peak, the company is now buried under a mountain of debt. As local Wuxi officials lured Suntech with big loans and subsidies, other Chinese provinces established solar industries of their own. After years of this, the industry was suffering from overcapacity, prices were slashed and margins fell. Li Junfeng, a senior adviser at China's state planning agency, says at least half of all solar capacity now needs to be shut down. "Overcapacity results in low-price competition; all industries experiencing overcapacity have this problem."

In fact, the Chinese solar-panel industry is only the most noticeable example of a broader industrial overcapacity. Its rise and fall has become a familiar pattern in China. Ambitious local Communist Party officials provide government money to businesses they hope will be success stories that can further their careers. In Wuxi, the party secretary who brought

Suntech to China, Yang Weize, was feted for his success in establishing the solar industry. Yang was promoted in 2010 to become the party secretary of Nanjing, one of China's largest cities. Such examples lead party officials to believe that attracting industry and development to their provinces is the surest path to success. "The bottom line is that officials who climb the [Communist] party ladder fastest are usually those who oversee the most flashy investment projects and the fastest growth," said Matthew Forney and Laila Khawaja of the research consultancy Fathom China.

Besides direct cash subsidies, many local authorities in China offer very cheap land, cheap credit, cut-rate energy and tax breaks for companies that will invest in their province. The result is a country awash with excess capacity, from cars and chemicals to electronics and steel. In a recent study, Usha and George Haley, US-based academics, examined the Chinese steel, glass, paper and automobile industries. The researchers found that "subsidies account for about 30 per cent of industrial output. Most of the companies we looked at would probably be bankrupt without subsidies."

Only about 80 per cent of the country's steel production capacity is being used. About one-third of cement facilities are lying idle. "The problem with subsidies everywhere is they tend to support activity, not outcomes, and they become more of a problem when they're just subsidising inefficiencies," says John Rice, vice-chairman of General Electric. "If you do that in perpetuity, it just increases the size of the anchor that drags down growth."

*

The Chinese economy exhibits many of the characteristics of an emerging economy heading into a debt problem: a period of excessive investment; capital allocation sometimes influenced by political rather than commercial criteria; and heavy debt (now as high as 200 per cent of GDP when the debts of local authorities and state-owned enterprises are included).

The recent investment boom has left a "capital overhang" (a large amount of unproductive investment and overcapacity) that will emerge when all of China's under-utilised assets result in non-performing loans on the balance sheets of the banks that financed them.

Opinions are mixed, but many commentators believe that China has passed the point of no return and a crash is inevitable. The legendary hedge-fund manager Jim Chanos is deeply pessimistic. "The coming bust in China's real-estate market will be a thousand times that of Dubai," he warns. Edward Chancellor, a global strategist for asset manager GMO, says the fall is inevitable. "I can't tell you precisely when the downturn will hit," he says.

> No one can. All I know is that China has all the earmarks of a classic mania that will end badly – a compelling growth story that seduces investors into ill-starred speculation, blind faith in the competence of Chinese authorities to manage through any cycle, and over-investment in fixed assets with inadequate returns facilitated by an explosion in credit.

While such sentiments have been voiced by investors on the fringes for some time, recognition that China's growth model is unsustainable is now shared by some of the world's most credible observers. In a major assessment of the Chinese economy last year, the International Monetary Fund reported that "since the global crisis, a mix of investment, credit and fiscal stimulus has underpinned activity. This pattern of growth is not sustainable and is raising vulnerabilities. While China still has significant buffers to weather shocks, the margins of safety are diminishing." Paul Krugman, a Nobel laureate and one of the world's most respected economists, says:

> The signs are now unmistakable: China is in big trouble. We're not talking about some minor setback along the way, but something more fundamental. The country's whole way of doing business, the economic system that has driven three decades of incredible growth, has reached its limits. You could say that the Chinese

model is about to hit its Great Wall, and the only question now is just how bad the crash will be.

If this is starting to sound dire, note a few pieces of good news. The first is that while an investment-led growth strategy always ends in a painful adjustment, it doesn't always end in disaster. Countries can unwind some of the policy distortions that led to excessive investment and eventually put their economies on a more balanced growth path. For example, the United States in the 1920s, Brazil in the 1960s and 1970s and a number of East Asian economies in the 1980s and 1990s all experienced painful adjustments following the bursting of their government-induced investment bubbles, but each pulled through and established a foundation for future growth and stability. In particular, Korea, Taiwan and Singapore emerged from the Asian crisis in 1997 as stronger economies and more democratic nations.

The second piece of good news is that China is in an extremely strong position to stave off economic crisis. In a weaker country a large volume of non-performing loans may result in a debt crisis. But with China's more than US$3 trillion of reserves, a more likely outcome is that the government will bail out its banks and reduce the rate of investment. This scenario might lead to a reduced rate of economic growth, but it would not necessary involve a financial crash.

The final piece of good news is that China's leaders understand the problem. In March 2007, the Chinese premier, Wen Jiabao, gave a press conference in which he outlined what came to be known as the doctrine of the "four uns": "My mind is focused on the pressing challenges … There are structural problems in China's economy, which cause unsteady, unbalanced, uncoordinated and unsustainable development."

In itself, this was an extraordinary frank statement by a Chinese leader. But Wen then went on to elaborate what he meant by each of these "uns":

Unsteady development means overheated investment as well as excessive credit supply and liquidity and surplus in foreign trade and international payments.

Unbalanced development means uneven development between urban and rural areas, between different regions and between economic and social development.

Uncoordinated development means that there is lack of proper balance between the primary, secondary and tertiary sectors and between investment and consumption. Economic growth is mainly driven by investment and export.

Unsustainable development means that we have not done well in saving energy and resources and protecting the environment.

Well before Western commentators began to bell the cat, China's leaders had acknowledged the problems created by their export- and investment-heavy economic model. The government recognises that its economic model is increasingly obsolete and intends to shift to a more balanced and sustainable growth path.

How to find such a path? As we saw earlier, economies are made up of three components: investment, consumption and exports. To rebalance its economy, China must slow down the rate of investment. But if investment slows, then overall economic growth will slow unless another part of the economy picks up the slack. We can rule out rapid growth from exports because there is limited scope for China to increase exports while economies in the rest of the world are relatively weak and costs in China are rising. So to rebalance its economy without letting growth fall, China will need to boost consumption. That means overhauling the entire economic policy apparatus and shifting the investment-led growth model into reverse. And this is exactly what the Chinese are now trying to do.

The new Chinese president, Xi Jinping, has already taken steps to effect the transition. Xi calls his vision the "China Dream." Since he coined the phrase in 2012, the concept has rarely been out of the newspapers, with state media unleashing a propaganda blitz extolling the virtues of the president's dream. So-called Dream Walls are ubiquitous in schools and universities, where students are encouraged to write down their own dreams. The China Dream is the culmination of fuxing, the Communist Party's goal of national rejuvenation.

The China Dream may encompass a broad-ranging vision for China's future, but first and foremost it's about getting rich. Specifically, the Dream targets the achievement of the "two 100s." The first 100 is the goal of entering the group of so-called high-income countries by 2021, the centenary of the Chinese Communist Party. High-income countries are defined by the World Bank as having income per capita of more than US$12,000, or roughly twice China's income today – so achieving this goal would require China to double incomes in seven years. The second 100 is catching up to the West and becoming a fully developed nation by about 2049, the centenary of the founding of the People's Republic. These goals weave the history of the Communist Party into the future aspirations of the nation.

Shifting from the investment-led growth model towards a more balanced, consumer economy is central to the China Dream. This is a seismic ideological shift for the Communist Party, which has always emphasised the good of the collective over that of individual citizens. The party recognises that to change its growth model, it will have to encourage the people's material aspirations. In this vein, Xi emphasises that the China Dream is "a dream of the whole nation, *as well as of every individual.*" The "personal Chinese Dream" focuses on the wellbeing of individual citizens. The mantra of investment-led growth was personal sacrifice for national progress; the new mantra is national progress through individual success. In the new regime, the materialism of the consumer is a virtue, not a vice.

The new regime has been quick to begin the transition away from the former model. First, Xi has moved to reduce unproductive investment by winding back the spree of local government developments. His directives have set off a burst of national introspection in recent months about whether Chinese municipal leaders and developers have gone too far in their manic reach for the skies. The *People's Daily* newspaper, a Communist Party mouthpiece, issued an editorial in August 2013 aimed squarely at local bureaucrats: "The vanity of some local government officials has determined the skylines of cities." Earlier this year, Xinhua news agency publicised statements of contrition by Zhou Benshun, party secretary in Hebei province. Zhou confessed to "paying too much attention to economic growth" rather than to the "quality of development." Xinhua quoted Zhou conceding that he had "chased short-term results" but now would "immediately implement economic system adjustments."

Second, China is acting to eliminate some of its excess industrial capacity, the legacy of decades of overinvestment. "We intend to ... vigorously adjust and optimise the economic structure," said Zhang Gaoli, the executive vice premier in charge of the economy. "We will strictly ban approvals for new projects in industries experiencing overcapacity and resolutely halt construction of projects that violate regulations." In particular, China's authorities plan to force the closure of steel mills. China's top banking regulator, Shang Fulin, said strict credit policies would be used to restructure the steel industry: "We will take active measures to encourage mergers and acquisitions." Hebei province has pledged to cut steel production by 30 per cent by 2017 to reduce air pollution and overcapacity.

Third, China has started to unwind some of the policies that diverted resources from consumption to investment and exports. Over the past few years, China has allowed the value of the yuan to increase. The IMF now estimates that it is just 5–10 per cent undervalued. As the government has allowed the yuan to come back in line with the market value, the trade surplus has shrunk and the growth of foreign currency reserves has slowed. China has also relaxed *hukou* restrictions, allowed wages to rise and begun to remove some of the restrictions on financial markets. All of these steps will help boost consumption and rebalance the economy.

Encouraged by these changes, some commentators believe China can and will shift to a more balanced path. "The fears are exaggerated," says Stephen Roach, Yale professor and former chief economist of Morgan Stanley. "China is going through a critical, once-in-twenty-years transition, to a different model of economic growth that will eventually be more balanced and more stable." Roach says that with the consumption share of the Chinese economy set to rise from 36 per cent of its GDP to as high as 60 per cent, "China is about to unleash the biggest consumer story that the world has ever seen."

The question is not whether China wants to change – it's whether it can. The early signs from the new government encouraged many, but the first step, weaning China off its addiction to debt-fuelled investment, will not be easy because it may mean a period of much slower growth. History teaches us that governments are reluctant to take away the punchbowl. "Quite simply," Michael Pettis says, "countries become addicted to high growth and low unemployment." The longer it takes China to abandon the economic policies that encourage excessive investment, the more capital will be wasted and the harder the economic transition to a more sustainable growth model. "China's leaders are riding a runaway train that they don't quite know how to stop," Patrick Chovanec says. "And they're running out of track."

*

Experts are divided on whether China's investment boom will end in a messy economic collapse or a passably smooth transition to a more balanced economy. The one thing everyone agrees on – including the Chinese themselves – is that the investment-led growth model cannot continue.

This is the critical point for Australia. Whichever path China takes, the resources-intensive investment boom will slow down, with consequences for our exports. If the transition founders, Chinese growth will slump and demand for Australian resources will rapidly slow. If the transition succeeds, consumption will replace investment as the main source of China's growth.

Either way, demand for resources will slow. This will have a significant impact on the prices of our main exports. In the past decade, China's growth caused demand for iron ore in particular to grow faster than supply, driving up the price. But now iron-ore prices face a double hit: Chinese demand is moderating just as supply increases.

The recent high prices caused many new mines to be opened and many existing mines to be expanded. By 2016, it is estimated, new iron-ore supply from Australia will have more than tripled since the boom began in earnest in 2004. And similar expansion is forecast in other major producing nations. Standard Chartered Bank predicted recently that the global deficit of iron ore, estimated at 77 million tonnes last year, would turn into a surplus of 136 million tonnes next year. Overcapacity, in other words, is an Australian problem too.

China's transition will mean falling prices for Australia's exports, rising prices for our imports and more competition for global capital. As these changes flow through to Australia, they will profoundly change our economy. The Reserve Bank governor, Glenn Stevens, said last year:

> It is hard to escape the feeling that we as a society have tended, for quite a long time now, to go about … making the assumption, perhaps without realising it, that solid growth of the economy will simply continue … We are at a moment now when that assumption has to be questioned.

Visitors to Melbourne in the 1880s were astonished. Here in the Southern Hemisphere was a dazzling metropolis superior to many European capitals.

They began to call it "Marvellous Melbourne." In just a decade, its progress had been astounding. The population more than doubled. Business boomed. Finance boomed. Humble buildings of the early colonists were pulled down, making way for ornate brick Romanesque-style commercial buildings in the centre of the city. New American elevators were imported to support construction of twelve-storey office towers on Collins Street that rivalled those in London and New York.

The construction boom extended into the suburbs. On the rolling hills of Kew and the flat paddocks of Brighton, opulent stone mansions were built for the newly rich. The building frenzy grew and fed upon itself until, by the mid-1880s, speculators had set off a full-blown land boom. Blocks selling in Surrey Hills for fifteen shillings a foot in 1884 rose to £15 in 1887. Land at Burwood rose in price from £70 to £300 an acre. Thousands of acres of suburban land were subdivided and resold many times, each time at a higher price. Auctioneers often provided free champagne at auctions.

By the 1880s Australia was the richest country in the world and Melbourne was its most magnificent city. In a now familiar pattern, the country's prosperity in the late nineteenth century was buoyed by a complementary economic relationship with a global power, which used Australia as a source of natural resources and a destination for surplus capital. Britain imported vast quantities of Australian wool, wheat and gold in the 1860s and 1870s, as well as dairy and meat following the introduction of refrigerated shipping in the 1880s. Australia's commodity exports to Britain were balanced by a torrent of financial capital flowing in the reverse direction. Britain was the world's largest source of capital and Australia was one of the biggest recipients of British investment.

In the 1880s boom, British capital financed nearly 40 per cent of Australian investment, fuelling bubbles in Australian stock markets, soaring property prices and a boom in imports of luxury goods. Despite the distance of more than a century, the parallels between Australia's relationship with Britain in the nineteenth century and with China today are not inconsiderable.

When the crash came, it caught the city by surprise. In 1891 Thomas Fallon made a trip to London to celebrate the successful completion of his architectural masterpiece. He had invested thousands of pounds to build the magnificent Queen Anne–style Wool Exchange building, situated beside the Rialto on Collins Street. As news of a financial panic in Melbourne broke, he rushed home to discover that not a single office in the new building could be let. According to a report in the *Argus* on 6 January 1892, boarders at the Salisbury house in Carlton heard two gunshots at half-past eight on Monday morning, following which Mr Fallon was discovered "lying on his bed with a revolver in his right hand and a hole in the right side of his head." In his pocket was a letter demanding he present himself at the Colonial Bank that morning.

As property prices fell and the stock market crashed, more than twenty major banks and financial institutions collapsed, wiping out the wealth of rich and poor alike. A gentleman by the name of Tommy Robertson had made a small fortune squatting around the Campaspe River. In 1890 he had visited all the building societies on Collins Street, making a meticulous list of the interest rates each was offering, and divided his life's savings among the six paying the highest rate. Two years later every one of the societies was bankrupt; Robertson regained not a penny and drowned himself in the Yarra.

At the end of 1892, conditions in Victoria were bleak. One newspaper reported that:

> Never before in the history of the colony has a Christmas holiday been shrouded in such deep gloom. Shopkeepers complain that their customers appeared to have forgotten that the season of good

cheer was at hand, and started on being asked for the accustomed order, as if reminded of the changed condition of their purses that does not admit of luxuries or extras.

Why did the boom end? And why was the crash so painful? The proximate cause of the downturn was the end of the twin resources booms that had fuelled Australia's growth for most of the century. Exports of gold slowed down as the accessible deposits dwindled across the goldfields of Victoria and New South Wales. At the same time, wool prices experienced a long decline which, along with a drought, savaged the profitability of Australian farming. As graziers felt financial pain in the 1890s, wool production fell 32 per cent and the nation's sheep population was culled from 106 million in 1892 to just 54 million in 1903.

As always, the shape of the crash was determined by the boom that preceded it. Australia had acted through the long nineteenth-century boom as if the windfall was permanent and the good times would never end. But our gold resources were finite and our wool wealth was leveraged to the vagaries of global commodity prices. When the gold ran out and the price of wool fell, our fall was both sudden and prolonged. As we saw earlier in this essay, Australia quickly dropped from top position in the world income rank in 1890 to ninth position by the turn of the century. It would take nearly fifty years for Australian real incomes to climb back to where they had been in 1890 – which is to say that Australians at the start of World War II were no wealthier in real terms than their grandparents had been.

In the nineteenth century, Australians didn't use the boom years to prepare for the future. We took favourable global circumstances for granted and mortgaged our prospects instead of preserving our prosperity. In his history of the Australian economy, Ian McLean wonders whether "Australians were consuming too much of the rent from resources extraction, and investing too little in alternative productive assets." Australians in the nineteenth century, he says, were "bringing forward their consumption of the bounty of the natural resources they had discovered without making full provision for the maintenance of their standards of living."

The question for Australians today is: if the China resources boom comes to an end, will we look back on the early twenty-first century with the same regret?

*

Australia's bountiful resources helped deliver tremendous prosperity in the twenty-first century, just as they did through much of the nineteenth century. In both periods Australia was lifted to the top of the global income ladder by buoyant commodity prices, a flexible economy and good governance. In both periods, the question has been asked: how do we maintain our prosperity when the boom times end?

The economics profession has clear insights to help countries manage their resources wealth for the long-term benefit of their people. The first insight is that resources need to be actively managed. Their mere existence doesn't guarantee prosperity; in fact, the discovery of resources often brings as much pain as gain. Diamonds brought perpetual war to Liberia, Sierra Leone, Côte D'Ivoire and Congo; oil brought corruption and stagnation to the economies of Venezuela, Nigeria and many other petroleum producers. "All in all, I wish we had discovered water," said Sheikh Ahmed Yamani of Saudi Arabia, a country whose wealth and poverty rates have stagnated for many decades despite vast reserves of oil. Natural resources often bring endemic economic volatility and frequently retard the development of other industries. The discovery of natural resources has failed to alleviate poverty in Angola, Bhutan, Congo, Iran, Algeria, Gabon, Belize, Ecuador, Guyana, Guatemala and many other countries.

The observation that many of the world's most resources-abundant countries are also among the world's poorest is known as the "resource curse." In 1995 Jeffrey Sachs and Andrew Warner investigated the resource curse using data for more than seventy countries over an eighteen-year period. They found that resources-abundant countries exhibited worse economic performance, on average, than countries without natural resources. This finding seems counter-intuitive: Why would resources-rich countries be poorer, on average, than countries without resources?

The curse was explained in the 1980s by Max Corden, one of Australia's most renowned economists. Corden showed that when a country's resources sector is booming, it can do long-term harm to other sectors of the economy. When the resources boom ends, the country has little to fall back on. In Corden's research this damage, which he called "Dutch Disease," occurs for two reasons.

First, a booming resources sector monopolises scarce capital and skilled workers. The other sectors shrink as their workers and funding leave to join the resources boom. This is called the "capability movement effect," because the economy's production capability (workers and capital) moves from one sector to another. We saw this effect at work in Cairns, when Darren lost his chef to the mines and had to close his restaurant on Monday and Tuesday nights. We also saw it in the Cairns tourism industry, which may suffer over the long term if investments are not made to renew and develop transport and accommodation.

Second, a booming resources sector harms other sectors by reducing their competitiveness. The resources boom brings extra wealth into the economy, pushing up the price of everything from haircuts to restaurant meals. But this "spending effect" then reduces the competitiveness of Australian goods relative to foreign goods because prices of domestic goods rise relative to those of goods made abroad. In Cairns we saw this effect in the rising prices that kept foreign tourists away. As the cost of meals, transport and accommodation in Australia went up, tourists looked to cheaper destinations. We also saw it at work in the local car industry, as the rising Australian dollar encouraged more of us to buy imported vehicles.

Dozens of countries have experienced the damaging impact of the capability movement and spending effects during a resources boom. Canada's rising dollar disadvantaged its manufacturing sector in the 2000s; Nigeria's discovery of oil reduced its agricultural capability in the 1990s;

there was the effect of North Sea Oil on UK manufacturing in the 1970s and 1980s, and the decline of the manufacturing sector in the Netherlands after the discovery of a large natural-gas field in 1959 – the original case of "Dutch Disease."

*

There are three remedies for Dutch Disease.

The first is to increase the flexibility of the economy. A flexible economy is able to withstand the capability movement effect because capital and workers can move more easily between sectors. Workers are pulled towards the mines during a resources boom, but when the boom passes they make the transition back to other sectors of the economy. In an inflexible economy the transition is more difficult, and the non-resources sectors are less resilient during the boom and slower to bounce back once it has passed.

In Australia economic flexibility is often narrowly defined as industrial relations, but the concept encompasses any policy that helps Australian workers and businesses adjust to changing economic circumstances. Flexibility is enhanced by improved education, lower trade barriers, the elimination of unnecessary regulation, improved worker mobility and greater entrepreneurial agility.

Over the past thirty years, both sides of politics have sought to make the Australian economy more flexible. Floating the dollar and cutting tariffs, as well as labour market and microeconomic reform across many industries, have reduced rigidities that would have impaired our response to global forces. The flexibility of our economy, particularly our exchange rate and monetary policy, helped us through the Asian financial crisis in the late 1990s and the global financial crisis in 2008. Flexibility also helped us adjust to the huge structural transformation brought about by China's boom – for instance, by aiding the massive shift of labour and capital into mining and related industries.

We will need more flexibility to adjust to the next phase of China's economic transformation. As we saw, there is considerable uncertainty over its future. The only safe bet is that China's economy will change dramatically and force Australia to change as well. Already, commodity prices have fallen, reducing our terms of trade by 14 per cent since their peak in 2011, leading to a fall in government revenue and the postponement of many resources projects. The hope is that falling investment in mining will be gradually offset by increased spending on housing, tourism and agriculture. But, as Glenn Stevens has said, the transition may "take some time yet and it will be against the backdrop of a challenging environment." Ross Garnaut puts the challenge more bluntly in his book *Dog Days*: "If we fail to take an early opportunity to adjust down the cost levels that have hung over from the China resources boom, we can look forward to economic instability, inflation, stagnation and high unemployment." Stevens calls for broad economic reform and says that of the "myriad things which can make it harder or easier for businesses to innovate, to change their ways of doing things, to avoid unnecessary costs and to be more productive, all matter. No single one is decisive in itself; but collectively, they are crucial."

The second remedy for Dutch Disease is to limit the spending effect. This can be achieved by saving, rather than spending, the proceeds of the boom. Increased saving limits the inflation of local prices, which are otherwise pushed up by the resources boom to the point where it becomes hard for local goods to compete with goods produced in other countries.

Unfortunately, Australia did not save much of the proceeds of the mining boom over the past decade. As the boom took off between 2004 and 2007, it added $334 billion in windfall gains to the budget. Australia saved only 6 per cent of this, using the remaining 94 per cent to fund tax cuts and spending increases, which amplified the spending effect by pushing up wages and prices and eroding the competitiveness of other industries.

Compare Australia's approach to that of Chile. Chile produces a third of the world's copper, making its economy and its government budget highly sensitive to the global price of copper. To insure against this, the government created a Copper Stabilisation Fund in 1985. Whenever the price of copper increased, the government would direct a proportion of the increased revenues into the fund; these resources would then be used during those years when the price of copper fell below the "ordinary" level. This fund helped Chile protect itself, at least partly, from the volatility of the copper market. Chile's approach helped the government to fend off spending pressures and run large surpluses as copper prices surged during the commodities boom of the 2000s. When the boom slowed, Chile had been posting big surpluses for several years, which in 2008 amounted to a savings war chest of 20 per cent of GDP.

In Australia the debate about saving our resources wealth often boils down to simplistic discussion of whether or not we should have a sovereign wealth fund. But this debate misses the main point. In a mining boom, the extra money sloshing through the economy causes Australian prices to go up, making Australian goods less competitive relative to foreign goods (that is, increasing the real exchange rate) and hurting the competitiveness of non-resources industries (what we referred to as the spending effect). In an economy suffering Dutch Disease, the purpose of stashing money away in a sovereign wealth fund is primarily to reduce spending today rather than to increase spending in the future. These objectives might sound like two sides of the same coin, but the distinction is important because what matters (and what should be targeted) is not how much a country saves, but how much it spends. The objective of Chile's system, for example, is not to maximise the accumulation of savings in the fund, but to ensure that government spending doesn't rise too much during the boom in a way that would damage the competitiveness of non-resources industries. In 2006 Chile passed the Fiscal Responsibility Law, which ensured that the government didn't spend the temporary benefits of commodity windfalls. Independent advisers were appointed to ensure that official forecasts could not be manipulated for political purposes or prone to over-optimism. Compare this to Australia, which created the Future Fund during our mining boom. The Future Fund was explicitly focused on future savings (in particular, it was supposed to meet the costs of public-sector superannuation liabilities), rather than on helping to stabilise the real exchange rate by limiting the spending effect from resources revenues. The Future Fund was a positive addition to Australia, but it was no substitute for sound fiscal rules, and it didn't prevent accelerating government spending and tax cuts from washing through the economy during the mining boom.

The third remedy for Dutch Disease is to make the non-resources industries in our economy more productive. The more productive such industries are, the more resilient they will be in the face of both the capability movement and spending effects.

To improve the productivity of our non-resources industries, we will have to broaden our relationship with Asia. As China changes, we should not let our economic ties diminish, but rather turn its transition to our advantage. We should increase our links with China and Asia's other growth engines – India, Korea and Indonesia. Australia has much to offer Asia's booming new middle classes, as they seek out a growing range of goods and services, from health and aged care to tourism, education, financial services, household goods and high-quality food. Australia can build and develop highly competitive industries in each of these areas.

Services are a clear opportunity. With our educated population, English language and attractive lifestyle, Australia is well placed to export services to Asia, particularly in law, finance and information technology. Sydney and Melbourne should be service centres for Asia that compete successfully with Singapore and Hong Kong. To do that, we need to create a competitive tax and regulatory regime, broaden and deepen our cultural and commercial partnerships across the region and become a more Asia-literate society.

Education is already Australia's largest services export sector, and there is scope for it to grow substantially. Asia has seen higher-education enrolment rates explode over the last thirty years. The number of outbound students from Asia has almost doubled over the past decade to more than a million, as many look abroad for international experience, cultural exchange and employment. Australia must continue to make it easy and attractive for Asian students to come here for high-quality education and work experience.

Australia should be a top tourist destination for Asia's middle classes as they increasingly look abroad for holidays. By 2030 there will be 541 million outbound tourists from the Asia-Pacific region. Australia's natural beauty and proximity give us a natural advantage in the global tourism market. To capitalise on this, we must improve our transport infrastructure and invest in world-class tourist facilities that are culturally relevant to Asian travellers.

Australia should be a preferred supplier of high-quality, good-value food for the Asian region. We need to protect and foster our global brand as a safe, natural environment free of biosecurity risks. We need to foster strong investment in research and development to align our products with Asia's consumption trends. We need greater investment to boost the competitiveness of our agricultural industries and better infrastructure to reduce the cost and increase the speed of transport. We must manage our natural resources, including soil, water and energy, in a way that sustains our farming over time. And finally, we should continue to use trade negotiations and intergovernmental engagement to promote freer trade in agricultural produce.

To capture these opportunities in the rapidly growing Asian market, Australia needs to focus on the basics of a productive economy. That means ensuring we maintain a world-class education system, modern infrastructure, incentives for innovation and growth, and a healthy population. Australia's egalitarian, open and resilient economy is the domestic platform for successful international engagement.

These three principles – maintaining flexibility, dampening the volatility caused by a resources boom and boosting the productivity of other sectors of the economy – should form the basis of Australia's economic framework.

The end of the China investment boom has brought Australia to a point of vulnerability all of our own making. We have allowed temporary wealth to wash through the economy, eroding the competitiveness of industries other than mining. Governments on both sides of politics have used the temporary revenues of the boom to fund permanent tax cuts and spending increases. We have failed to prepare our economy and our people for life after the boom.

Is it too late to change? Now that China is in transition, has the horse already bolted? The answer is that it is never too late. Australia has great strengths beyond resources, including a well-educated workforce, world-leading institutions, a multicultural community and an open economy. If we build a policy framework that is flexible, prepare our economy to ride out the volatility of global circumstances, and position ourselves to take advantage of the opportunities afforded by Asia's rise, Australia can continue to prosper.

THE PARADOX OF PROSPERITY

Australia's ambassador in Beijing, Geoff Raby, had decorated the embassy with the vivid art of Chinese-Australian painters, including Lin Chunyan and Guan Wei. Their canvases are colourful paeans to cross-cultural mixture, blending Australian and Chinese motifs. Both came to Australia around the time of Tiananmen. They and dozens of other Chinese painters, sculptors, writers, musicians and poets were able to remain in Australia after Bob Hawke's tearful decision, on 9 June 1989, to override his bureaucrats and relax Australia's visa laws.

Twenty years have passed since Lin and Guan came to Australia. Had they been in the ambassador's dining room as the prime minister and his guests discussed the future of their two nations, they could not have helped but be struck by the historical symmetry of the unfolding events. Over two decades China has changed beyond recognition, stepping up to take its place as an economic, political and cultural superpower. The global interest in Chinese contemporary art is "a symbol of China's emergence as a member of the global community," Geoff Raby says. China's rise has changed the world, a transformation that has suddenly become the all-absorbing topic for those professionally concerned with the future of the planet.

In 2008 one of Lin's landscapes was hanging in the ambassador's dining room above the guests assembled for the prime minister's banquet. At first glance the painting seems to be of an Australian forest, but, as Raby explains, the colours aren't truly Australian: "the more you look at it, the more you realise it's not ... So there is something else happening there. There is another eye. There is another perspective. I think this is the Chinese perspective – a foreign eye looking at an Australian landscape." Lin's distinctive imagery reflects themes of identity and discovery; he sees Australia as a traveller moving between the ancient world and the new world.

Australians never seem fully comfortable with our place in the world. We don't try too hard to explain our prosperity, preferring to put it down to our status as the Lucky Country. Ascribing our situation to chance avoids the difficult task of explaining our prosperity. It also betrays the fact that our success is often caused by factors outside our control.

This insecurity is the conceit behind the Lucky Country. On any objective measure, Australia has been a success. But it's the subjective that haunts us. On that measure, Australia has only seldom, and never for long, felt truly secure in the wider world. We survived global and domestic upheavals, but we have never felt that we have "made it" as a nation, in the sense of having a common understanding of the source of our success and being comfortably confident of continuing it into the future. We have never felt that we've really arrived, the *fait* is never *accompli*.

This is the paradox of Australia's prosperity. We are successful, but our wealth feels insecure. We can be among the richest nations in the world and one of the least competitive at the same time. We can slip from boom to bust within a few years. We can be both a "banana republic" and a "miracle economy" in the space of two decades. We can be derided as the "poor white trash of Asia" and lauded as the richest nation in the world within a generation.

This perennial uncertainty shouldn't be a surprise to Australians. The conclusion, obvious from our brief review of economic history, is that uncertainty is an inherent feature of our circumstances. As a small, open, resources-abundant economy, we should accept that our fortune will, to some extent, always be leveraged to global conditions. Our fate will never be fully in our own hands and we will be perpetually mining our prosperity from a thin seam of the global economy. This is the hard edge of the Lucky Country – Australia's success will always depend on an element of luck. Our challenge is to manage this luck over the long term.

Few periods have been luckier for Australia than the two decades of China's industrialisation. As the world's most mineral-rich continent, sitting right on China's doorstep, Australia has been well placed to supply the raw materials China can't do without. We were among the biggest beneficiaries of China's manic manufacture of steel vertebrae for everything from

Never again miss an issue. Subscribe and save.

☐ **1 year subscription** (4 issues) $59 (incl. GST). Subscriptions outside Australia $89.
All prices include postage and handling.

☐ **2 year subscription** (8 issues) $105 (incl. GST). Subscriptions outside Australia $165.
All prices include postage and handling.

☐ Tick here to commence subscription with the current issue.

PAYMENT DETAILS I enclose a cheque/money order made out to Schwartz Publishing Pty Ltd.
Or please debit my credit card (MasterCard, Visa or Amex accepted).

CARD NO. ☐☐☐☐ ☐☐☐☐ ☐☐☐☐ ☐☐☐☐

EXPIRY DATE   /   CCV   AMOUNT $

CARDHOLDER'S NAME

SIGNATURE

NAME

ADDRESS

EMAIL   PHONE

tel: (03) 9486 0288 **fax:** (03) 9486 0244 **email:** subscribe@blackincbooks.com **www.quarterlyessay.com**

An inspired gift. Subscribe a friend.

☐ **1 year subscription** (4 issues) $59 (incl. GST). Subscriptions outside Australia $89.
All prices include postage and handling.

☐ **2 year subscription** (8 issues) $105 (incl. GST). Subscriptions outside Australia $165.
All prices include postage and handling.

☐ Tick here to commence subscription with the current issue.

PAYMENT DETAILS I enclose a cheque/money order made out to Schwartz Publishing Pty Ltd.
Or please debit my credit card (MasterCard, Visa or Amex accepted).

CARD NO. ☐☐☐☐ ☐☐☐☐ ☐☐☐☐ ☐☐☐☐

EXPIRY DATE   /   CCV   AMOUNT $

CARDHOLDER'S NAME   SIGNATURE

NAME

ADDRESS

EMAIL   PHONE

RECIPIENT'S NAME

RECIPIENT'S ADDRESS

tel: (03) 9486 0288 **fax:** (03) 9486 0244 **email:** subscribe@blackincbooks.com **www.quarterlyessay.com**

Delivery Address:
37 LANGRIDGE St
COLLINGWOOD VIC 3066

Quarterly Essay
Reply Paid 79448
COLLINGWOOD VIC 3066

Delivery Address:
37 LANGRIDGE St
COLLINGWOOD VIC 3066

No stamp required
if posted in Australia

Quarterly Essay
Reply Paid 79448
COLLINGWOOD VIC 3066

cars and trucks to railways, apartments and office towers. China was a big reason why Australia's economy has grown by 4 per cent a year for about twenty years, why we avoided the Asian financial crisis in the 1990s, why our house prices rose in the 2000s, why global financial imbalances crashed the global economy in 2008, and why Australia alone among the major nations escaped the ensuing recession.

Understanding China's growth model helps explain why Australia has done so well in the twenty-first century. But it also explains why, at the same time, our economic anxiety is reaching a zenith: why Holden is leaving, why the budget is in such an apparent quagmire, why house prices are soaring, why the dollar is so volatile. China's growth has brought us a windfall, but it is a precarious sort of prosperity.

We haven't helped ourselves in this regard. In the boom years, Australians embraced the windfall of China's growth without preparing for the aftermath. We allowed the non-mining economy to wither and failed to save resources profits. As a nation, we have to be smarter than this. If we are happy to leave our prosperity to luck, we can continue to bob up and down on the tide of global circumstance; but if we want to be a successful country, we need to learn to surf the waves.

SOURCES

9   "Over the last twenty years, Australia's economic growth": Between 1993 and
     2013, the Japanese economy grew by 25 per cent. Over the same period the
     European economy grew faster, being 33 per cent larger after twenty years.
     Among the best-performing economies, the British economy expanded by just
     over 50 per cent and the American economy grew by 66 per cent to finish the
     two decades two-thirds larger than it started. By contrast, the Australian econ-
     omy grew by more than 90 per cent over the same period.

9   "little hope was held for our economic future": Ian Macfarlane, 2006 Boyer
     Lectures.

9   "goal of reaching the top ten nations": *Australia in the Asian Century*, white paper,
     October 2012: "For Australia to reach the top 10 by 2025, all else being equal,
     Australia's labour productivity growth needs a boost of about one-half of a per-
     centage point a year above the 'business as usual' scenario."

10   "Australians had become the seventh-richest": Measured by the World Bank in
     2012 as gross national income per capita (Atlas method) at market exchange
     rates.

14   "one enormous goldfield": *Scottish Farmer*, 16 August 1851, "Latest News from
     the Gold Mines."

16   "staggering 19 per cent of the world's total known mineral wealth": World
     Bank, *The Changing Wealth of Nations: Measuring Sustainable Development in the New Millen-
     nium*, The International Bank for Reconstruction and Development, Washing-
     ton, DC, 2011.

17   "second-richest nation on the planet by natural wealth per capita: ibid.

24   "the yuan was 20–25 per cent undervalued": Morris Goldstein, Peterson Insti-
     tute for International Economics, and Nicholas R. Lardy, Peterson Institute for
     International Economics, "China's Currency Needs to Rise Further," op-ed in
     the *Financial Times*, 22 July 2008.

25   "It's a new world for us in the city": Ian Johnson, "China's Great Uprooting,"
     The New York Times, 15 June 2013.

26   "All I wanted at that time was to move to the city": Liyan Qi, "Hukou Holdup,"
     The Wall Street Journal, 9 November 2013.

27   "deposit rates were set at just 0.72 per cent": Figures in this section come from
     Nicholas R. Lardy, "Financial Repression in China," Peterson Institute for Inter-
     national Economics, policy brief, September 2008.

30   "Darren, the proprietor for many years": Darren is not the subject's real name.
     At his request, his name and that of the business have been changed.

30   "this region has lost much of its 'punch'": Cairns Mayor Bob Manning, address to Cairns Regional Council, 16 May 2012.

32   "the price of Forrest's Fortescue Metals Group stock": This calculation takes the FMG share split into account.

35   "up nearly 80 per cent": S&P 500 rose 80.2 per cent from September 2002 to September 2007.

35   "British FTSE – up 70 per cent": FTSE 100 rose 67.5 per cent from September 2002 to September 2007.

35   "All Ordinaries index to more than double": All Ordinaries index rose 116 per cent from September 2002 to September 2007.

35   "more than 50 million people": International Labor Organisation, *World of Work Report 2012*.

54   "High-income countries are defined": Note that the threshold for "high-income countries" is around $12,600. The thresholds are measured by the World Bank according to its Atlas method, which smooths exchange-rate fluctuations over a multi-year period. China actually describes its goal in terms of becoming a "moderately wealthy country," which is not a recognised classification but is widely assumed to refer to the World Bank's "high income" categorisation.

57   "It is hard to escape the feeling": Glenn Stevens, Opening Statement to House of Representatives Standing Committee on Economics, 18 December 2013.

58   "The construction boom extended into the suburbs": Figures in this section from Michael Cannon, *The Land Boomers*, Melbourne University Press, Melbourne, 1966.

59   "Never before in the history": *Table Talk*, 1892.

60   "Australian real incomes to climb back": Figures from Ian Mclean, *Why Australia Prospered: The Shifting Sources of Economic Growth*, Princeton University Press, Princeton, NJ, 2013.

61   "economics profession has clear insights": See the research of P. Collier, A. J. Venables, F. van der Plog, J. W. Gunning, W. M. Corden and others. Note that much of this literature is written in the context of development economies and typically focuses on economies less advanced than Australia's. Nonetheless, many of the tenets are applicable to rich and poor countries alike.

61   "resources-abundant countries exhibited worse economic performance": The existence of the resource curse is disputed. Early work (including Jeffrey D. Sachs and Andrew M. Warner, "Natural Resource Abundance and Economic Growth," National Bureau of Economic Research Working Paper No. 5398, Cambridge, MA, 1997) has been disputed by recent contributions (Tiago

Cavalcanti, Kamiar Mohaddes and Mehdi Raissi, "Commodity Price Volatility and the Sources of Growth," Cambridge Working Papers in Economics, 2011).

67   "By 2030 there will be 541 million": *Australian in the Asian Century*, white paper.

Mary Crock

Paul Toohey's essay is striking in the accuracy of his cameo sketches of the individuals using Indonesia as a staging post in their efforts to seek sanctuary in Australia. His largely sympathetic portrayal of the asylum seekers with whom he interacted confirms my assessment that the vast majority of those who risk their lives in a boat crossing to Australia have at least arguable protection claims. Of course, no collection of asylum seekers represents a monolithic group. It has always been the case that asylum flows comprise individuals who range from the most exquisitely vulnerable to plain-faced opportunists who are simply out for a quick result – or, failing that, a quick turnaround. In recent years I have also encountered individuals who claimed – and whom I believe – they were duped by smooth-talking smugglers into believing they were pursuing a regular migration option when buying their ticket to Australia.

In the course of fieldwork in Cisarua my research team and I encountered Afghan, Sri Lankan, Iranian, Burmese and other asylum seekers who were negotiating the uncertainties and vicissitudes of life as undocumented migrants in a foreign land. Most were relative newcomers to Indonesia, although a sizeable cohort of those we interviewed were longer-term residents living in accommodation supported by the UN High Commissioner for Refugees' implementing partners. Some were dealing with grief and injuries sustained in attempting to make the perilous sea crossing to Australia. I remain haunted by the case of an eight-year-old boy who had survived a shipwreck that took the life of his uncle and guardian. He was living with a lovely family of refugees who had opened their tiny home and hearts to him. As the family had been selected for resettlement in New Zealand, the boy's future was uncertain.

Like Toohey, we met with a young man who casually gave us the details of the top smugglers operating in the region. He, too, was angry with and disdainful of this group. We heard accounts of breathtaking corruption: of one lane of a highway being closed to traffic so that a bus carrying asylum seekers could travel unimpeded through south Jakarta to the coast, a drive of over three hours on a clear road. We heard of so many boats foundering at sea that we gained the impression that many of the asylum seekers may have been just as safe playing Russian roulette. I would defy anyone who spends any time in this part of the world to come away feeling warm and comfortable about the character and methods of the smugglers who profit from this trade in human misery.

What is refreshing about Toohey's work is that the author has descended from the high towers of the commentariat to go and see what is really happening on the ground. This will always be useful as it brings home the messiness of the human condition, demonstrating that simple constructions of a devilishly complicated problem will rarely deliver sustainable solutions. Toohey's critique of our politicians is generally a fair one. Labor's response to the phenomenon did indeed indicate a lack of conviction and confusion. The frequent policy changes, the attempts to bring about a decisive deal-breaker with the Malaysia Solution and then the Expert Panel, were poorly conceived and poorly executed.

I share Toohey's concern that the approach taken by the current government does not look sustainable in the longer term. This is borne out by the prime minister's cancelling a planned trip to Indonesia because of "on-water" operations (code for the push-back of another asylum-seeker boat). However, noting that Tony Abbott and Scott Morrison have treated Indonesia with less respect than that great nation deserves is only part of the problem. What begins as an engaging discussion of an issue that seems to transfix Australians finishes somewhat lamely with a suggestion that Kevin Rudd perhaps showed better understanding of the polycentric nature of the issue within our region. There are no grand suggestions for a better way forward.

Toohey fails to capture the extent to which Australian law, policy and practice have moved into the territory of the extreme. The manner in which we are placing the lives of men, women and children at risk is beyond the pale. The amount of money expended to support our abusive practices – and the fact that it is leached from our foreign-aid budget – is obscene.

There can be no debate now that Australia is blatantly acting in breach of its obligations under international law. No dispute that our behaviour offends the most basic standards of human decency. We are creating a new subclass, with thousands living in the community with no right to work or rebuild their lives, and recent arrivals punished with indefinite detention. We send men, women and children to live in conditions that the UN has described as inhuman and degrading. Under Labor, many of the women shipped to Manus Island who fell pregnant lost their babies because of the anti-malarial drugs administered to them. At least one asylum seeker sent to this hellhole has been killed (some would argue, murdered); a number now live in fear for their lives. None of this becomes Australia – a state that otherwise more than pulled its weight in creating and maintaining the international framework for the protection of human rights.

Like so much of the discourse in this country, Toohey's discussion of the legalities surrounding our treatment of asylum seekers is one-dimensional. He spends some time in his essay digressing to discuss the proper way to describe the people who are trying so hard to enter Australia. Are they illegals or asylum seekers or refugees? The elements of international law on this point are interesting but not particularly helpful. In 1948 the Universal Declaration of Human Rights included at Article 14 a statement that every human being has the right to seek and to enjoy asylum from persecution. But such declarations are aspirational – not "hard" law. The Refugee Convention of 1951 established perhaps the most important principle and obligation of refugee law when it created the prohibition against the return or "refoulement" of Convention refugees. However, the instrument is silent on the critical issue of getting into a country in the first place to claim protection. This is the quandary facing refugees – they have no legal "right" to enter a country of refuge, only a right not to be sent away once they have entered.

Under Australian domestic law, any non-citizen entering without a visa becomes "unlawful." In Australia, one could therefore label undocumented asylum seekers "illegal." However, until such people cross the border onto Australian territory, the language of illegality is nonsense. People who have no visas to enter Australia can hardly be "illegals" until they enter Australia. In Indonesia, most of "our" asylum seekers enter and remain on temporary visas that are purchased upon arrival at the airport. Most are not at that stage irregular migrants.

I find the term "illegals" offensive because it is used typically to inflame adverse sentiments against individuals who historically and statistically do not deserve to be so victimised. An excellent example is its use by Toohey's "sober critic" Derek Parker, writing in *The Spectator*. It does mystify me that Australians are so hung up both on this language and on the phenomenon of irregular maritime arrivals – as I prefer to call them. Even in America and Europe, where irregular migration is endemic, asylum seekers do not attract anything like the opprobrium and angst we see in Australia.

On the issue of status, Toohey slips into the language used by politicians like Bob Carr, alleging that asylum seekers such as the late Reza Berati are not refugees, but fortune seekers in pursuit of economic advancement. Without assessing their claims, such statements are decidedly unhelpful. In the mouths of politicians they are self-serving, given Australia's first-order obligation to determine the status of any asylum seeker. The simple point missed in this discussion is that Australia's obligations to these people do not turn solely on their status as refugees. The right to life, the right to be treated decently – in fact, all manner of rights recognised under international law – inhere in all of us because of our shared humanity. Reza Barati did not deserve exile and torture. He did not deserve to die.

One other aspect of Toohey's essay that needs attention is where he refers to Amanda Vanstone's endorsement of the "Cone of Silence" Morrison and Abbott lowered upon taking office over the whole issue of boat arrivals. Vanstone's complaint was that the media's sympathetic coverage of asylum seekers had been playing into the hands of the smugglers, "pressing our sympathy button until we can't stand it any more."

I agree with Vanstone that media coverage of boat arrivals in Australia was a factor in the steep increase in boat arrivals after 2008. My complaint is that no one has called out the conservatives on the cynical role that they played in disrupting governmental attempts to dissuade people from resorting to the smugglers. In 2010 I spoke at a forum with (now Minister) Scott Morrison, arguing that the surge in boat arrivals was being encouraged, if not driven, by the then Opposition's cant about loss of control of Australia's borders. Who can forget the billboard trucks circling Perth with the number of boat arrivals clicking over? Neither Morrison nor the media present gave any quarter, insisting on the propriety of maintaining a lively public discourse on this issue.

The world is now interconnected as never before in human history. One of the most striking features of the asylum seekers we met in Indonesia was their awareness of global political events. We visited a shelter for unaccompanied children identified by UN agencies as asylum seekers. The young people all had mobile phones. All were connected to the internet. The bolder ones asked to "friend" me on Facebook – and they subsequently did, providing fascinating insight into how they projected themselves to the world. Interviewed as a group, all but one stated that the decision to travel to Indonesia had been made by a family member abroad. All bar one confirmed that the decision to get on a boat bound for Australia would be made by a relative overseas. Importantly, virtually all admitted to having family friends or acquaintances in Australia and accepted this as a reason for the choice of destination.

The starting point for policy debate on irregular migration should acknowledge the human chains that often influence the direction of migratory flows. What we do and say in Australia clearly does influence decisions made abroad.

At the same time, it is utterly unacceptable for a developed country like Australia to be engaging in behaviour that places the lives of vulnerable people at risk. It is incorrect that abject (criminal) cruelty is the only option going forward.

Toohey's ultimately rather tepid critique of what has really become a sorry situation captures what I see as the worst aspect of our national discourse on asylum seekers at the moment. The bipartisan hand-wringing about the need to "stop the boats to stop the terrible loss of life at sea" impresses few outside the country. Our policies are seen for what they are: the expression of a deep-seated fear and suspicion of those who come across the seas, and of a growing national selfishness.

Mary Crock

Mary Crock acknowledges the assistance of Ron McCallum, Hannah Martin and Daniel Ghezelbash with this response.

Michael Bachelard

I arrived in Jakarta in December 2011 to be Fairfax Media's Indonesia correspondent just as the number of boat-borne asylum seekers heading for Australia
exploded.

In the year before I arrived, just over 5000 people had come on boats, mainly
from Java's southern coast on the familiar route to Christmas Island. In 2011–12
it was 7300. In 2012–13, though, 18,119 people took the journey. Boats were
leaving every second day and thousands flooded into Indonesia from Iran,
Afghanistan, Sri Lanka to board them.

As the demand increased, so did the supply of smugglers wanting to make a
buck. For all their cynicism, the old smugglers had reputations to protect and were
interested in repeat business. The new crop, by contrast, were fly-by-nights, chas-
ing maximum profits. The quality of the boats fell as their number increased, and
more asylum seekers were robbed. Many of the new smugglers were themselves
only stopping briefly on their way to Australia. Some responded to the competition by sending ever bigger, more overcrowded boats as a marketing ploy.

The sinking in December 2010 on the rocks off Christmas Island had opened
the eyes of Australians to the potential for disaster, and another two boats which
went down off Java in November and December 2011, killing 230 passengers,
shocked people. But these tragedies did nothing to deter new passengers nor
shame the smugglers. In 2012 there were eight sinkings; in 2013 fourteen more
boats went down, drowning some or all on board.

But what wasn't clear in early 2012 was that the political response from Australia would be such a tragic combination of ineptitude and cynicism.

Labor's asylum policy for eighteen months lurched from one unconvincingly
tough position to another, and thanks to the High Court's 2011 ruling on the
Malaysia Solution and Tony Abbott's political gamesmanship, Canberra's attempt
to have any stance at all eventually sputtered out.

Australian policy was foundering and, as Paul Toohey points out in *That Sinking Feeling*, the then Opposition, dedicated to demonising Julia Gillard, wanted it that way.

On the ground the situation grew increasingly awful.

My first encounter with desperate people came in April 2012. A group of 120 asylum seekers had been rescued from the ocean by a commercial vessel and brought back to Indonesia's port of Merak, but they refused to disembark.

The stand-off lasted only a day – Indonesian authorities had learnt a lot from the months-long stalemates involving the *Oceanic Viking* and another boat at Merak in 2009, so they denied food, shelter and toilets to those on deck. In the late afternoon, they dragged the weakened men from the vessel.

I recall their screams. I had never heard men making such sounds. Two of them seized loose steel objects from the ship's deck and beat themselves over the head as police forced them, bloodied, off the boat.

In the following months, worse was to come. In August, I reported the fate of ten-year-old Omid Jafary. He'd watched his father, his uncle and his cousin die around him, sinking beneath the waves as he clung to the flotation device of another passenger. Then he was picked up and returned to Indonesia. Almost 100 died that day.

Later that year I spent time with the miracle survivor of another sinking. Habib Ullah had watched his thirty-three shipmates sink into the ocean over the course of about three days, until he was the only one left.

And still the boats came. The ocean was littered with death, but the numbers taking the chance ratcheted up relentlessly.

As Toohey movingly points out in the most powerful passages of his essay, the death and grief were hard to bear and, at times, it became difficult to maintain a reporterly distance.

All this tragedy prompted furious political activity in Australia, but none of it achieved anything. Like Toohey, I couldn't escape the feeling that crocodile tears were being shed. It seemed from this side of the ocean that Australia's politicians and their boosters were motivated mainly by their own political advantage or survival, not the welfare of asylum seekers. Since Howard, the Right had found the dislike of "irregular maritime arrivals" a rich vein to mine, but the only acceptable way to prosecute its case was to cloak this political calculation in concern over deaths at sea. Meanwhile, where the Right was organised, the Left was divided and ineffectual.

To most voters, I suspect, the drownings that came after Christmas Island in 2010 began to seem rather remote and theoretical, while successful arrivals were regarded almost as a personal affront.

The 100 per cent deterrence policy of the Abbott government has had its effect. Ask anyone in the asylum-seeker staging post of Cisarua now and they'll say, "The way is closed." They believe Tony Abbott and Scott Morrison where they never believed Kevin Rudd and Julia Gillard.

The boats still occasionally leave, but without much hope of success, and not since December 2013 have I had to report a drowning. My stories now are about the people who have been towed back or returned in bulbous orange lifeboats, and who emerge angry and bewildered right where they began – injured, some of them with burnt hands, for example, but alive.

I've reported the desperate alternatives some are seeking – the even more dangerous passage to New Zealand, the proposed plane flights (involving false documents or corrupt officials), the return home (particularly by the Iranians, many of whom quietly admit that they never belonged as refugees in the first place).

Now, though, most wait in Indonesia for resettlement through the so-called front door. This has its own problems, including lengthy detention in squalid, sometimes violent detention centres. Processing takes an undefined (and lengthening) period and can lead to desperate sadness. Mohammad Sarwar Hussaini chose the official route after I warned him in 2012 of the danger of the boat voyage, but he was later inexplicably rejected by Australia. He remains in no-man's-land.

In these ways, the change of government has changed everything. But it hasn't changed how I see my job – to report what happens to the human beings who are the subject of Australia's posturing. Even if the end justifies our country's policy means, we should at least know what the means are.

What has changed, though, is the barracking from the sidelines. Now when I write about a turn-back or an allegation of abuse, or the difficulty of life in the queue, my employer, Fairfax, and I are accused by the Right of being dewy-eyed apologists for "illegals." After I interviewed asylum seekers with burnt hands, @Riverrovks tweeted: "For god sake use some common sense. Maybe you should adopt these lying scum bags and use your money to look after them."

A favourite line of attack is the question, asked sneeringly: "Where were you when people were drowning?" I was dockside, but I'd be willing to bet that my accusers were sitting comfortably at home, barracking for the then Opposition to block any attempt by Labor to legislate to slow the frequency of boats.

But while the Right can be accused of hypocrisy, the Left seems keen to downplay the drownings. Its view of a compassionate approach means Australia should accept most of those who arrive by boat. Perhaps 1000 people, possibly more, have drowned trying to get to Australia over recent years and Australia's acceptance of the vast majority was essentially encouraging them to take the chance. Look into the eyes of young Omid Jafary and tell me there's anything compassionate about whole families dying at sea.

Radical global economic inequality, the religious and cultural persecution of minorities, ongoing war and extremism – all the things that make parts of the world awful places to live – are driving people out looking for a better place. Australia is a better place, and there is a well-established route to get there.

If the past few years have shown anything, it's that push factors and pull factors both exist. Without establishing some controls in Australian policy, and projecting those policies out to the potential customers of people smugglers, the numbers arriving by boat and seeking residency would, in my view, continue to increase.

Part of the tragedy is that Australian politics does not allow a sensible discussion about whether our society could bear 30,000, 50,000 or even 200,000 refugees per year through UN resettlement. Under Abbott, the intake has been reduced to 13,750. But if we opened the front door wider, would this encourage the people smugglers and chancers to multiply again, the economic migrants to jam in their foot, the drownings to recommence?

If there is a solution which does not involve the cruelty of indefinite offshore detention in dangerous camps, we are yet to discover it. Australia should surely be able to control its borders without being a renowned abuser of human rights. I suspect, though, that there are many Australians who both deplore the treatment of asylum seekers on Manus Island and Nauru and secretly hope it will ward off new arrivals.

Toohey's suggestion is for an Indonesian Solution. It may well be, as he says, the gold standard of such an idea, and it does seem inexplicable that no Australian government has made any serious attempt to negotiate one. But Toohey does not really spell out what the details might be. How, for example, could you settle more people in Australia, via Indonesia, without firing up the pull factors again? What number can Australia bear? Would more arrivals throw us back into political chaos and division? Since 2001, a large number of arrivals has reliably brought out the worst in our natures.

Addressing any of these questions seems well beyond the capacity of either the government or the Opposition of 2014.

I don't have any answers either, but I'll keep reporting the human fallout. Toohey's essay is both a handy reminder of where we've been and a moving testament to the same impulse – the desire to bear witness to a tragedy that's partly of Australia's making.

Michael Bachelard

| Correspondence

Neil James

A strength of Paul Toohey's essay is his understanding, all too rare, that asylum and refugee matters are, first and foremost, strategic policy issues with domestic ramifications, not vice versa. Toohey grasps the context: they comprise just one part of Australia's wider, complex and longer-term strategic relationships within our region and especially with Indonesia.

Public argument, on the other hand, has long been skewed and often been led nowhere by the contextual error of treating asylum seeking as a wholly domestic matter, whether politically, socially or morally. This fixates on the symptoms (refugee flows) rather than their causes (conflict, globalisation, economic disparities, selective take-up of Refugee Convention responsibilities) and the solutions (such as conflict resolution, true Convention burden-sharing). Argument is also generally fuelled by emotion and ideology, leading to simplistic analyses and reflexive moral condemnation, rather than engagement of opposing argument.

The refreshing objectivity of Toohey's essay stems from his detailed on-the-ground research in Indonesia and general knowledge of that country, his broader knowledge of how Australia's distinctive geostrategic and socioeconomic settings remain so central to the issue and his, frankly unusual, willingness to test the simplistic slogans that infest all sides of public argument about asylum-seeking issues. This enables him to dismantle many shibboleths regularly advanced in refugee advocacy and the equally simplistic nostrums common among those proposing hardline solutions.

Geostrategically, Australia is the only continent that is both an island and wholly the territory of one country. Australia is also the driest populated continent and is consequently both sparsely peopled and environmentally fragile. Geopolitically, Australia is a stable, first-world, liberal democracy with a widely accepted culture of mass immigration as a path to citizenship, but one located in near and wider regions where such standards of governance, living and openly acquired nationality are not the norm.

For those seeking asylum, Australia can be reached only by crossing the sea, either by authorised or unauthorised means. We are also effectively the only genuine signatory to the Refugee Convention in our immediate region, and one of only two such signatories among the thirty-five or so countries between the Arafura and Aegean seas.

The intrinsically uncontrollable nature of unauthorised arrival by boat – rather than the act of claiming asylum itself – is surely what underlies most community concern about this type of arrival. This is borne out by the markedly lesser concern about those asylum claimants arriving by authorised means, such as scheduled flight or ship, where much greater national control is possible.

Opinion polls consistently show that around four in five Australians consider that controlling illegal immigration should be an important goal of our foreign (and not just domestic) policy, but that fewer than one in ten believe that race should be an immigration criterion. Australia is also now a quite diverse society with extensive first-hand experience of immigration at family level. Rather than supposed xenophobia or ignorance, the true bedrock of community attitudes about unauthorised arrivals remains reasoned appreciation of the potential risk for ever-growing numbers, if uncontrolled, to compromise Australia's national immigration policy, sovereignty and perhaps eventually – should numbers increase – our domestic economic, social and political stability.

No matter whether community perceptions of "queue-jumping" are valid or not – nor whether a UNHCR queue exists or not (however imperfectly) – some public claims about "boat people" are undoubtedly due to misunderstandings. A common one stems from confusion about who is an asylum seeker and who is an illegal immigrant, which can only be determined ex post facto and often long after their unauthorised but not necessarily illegal arrival.

However, Australians generally seem to feel that asylum claimants need to prove the validity of their claims in case they are fraudulently seeking an immigration outcome and taking the place of a genuine refugee. Much single-issue refugee advocacy, on the other hand, seems to assume that all or most asylum claimants are automatically genuine refugees needing protection. This approach assumes that even though highly desired permanent residence and eventually citizenship is usually the outcome, little or no immigration fraud should be suspected, deterred, countered or punished.

Arguments in favour of accepting all or at least more asylum seekers almost invariably centre on the low numbers currently arriving. This ignores legitimate concerns about Australia's lack of control over the process. Even more illogically, it does nothing to assuage general appreciation about the risk of larger or even unsustainable numbers if policy remains so hostage to events.

Concern about Australia, almost alone in the region, having to face the risk of much higher numbers of arrivals also seems to be why so many Australians are sceptical when it is argued that onshore processing of asylum claims in Australia does not result in a significant "demand-pull" effect.

Media coverage of asylum-seeking often ignores these geopolitical and geostrategic contexts. Instead, it features only simplistic quotes from a refugee advocate or two and the relevant minister. This has four unhelpful effects.

First, such superficial coverage reduces the issue to a party-political contest or a morality-based blood sport, which hampers resolution of the practical and moral dilemmas involved.

Second, it fails to challenge the intellectual gaps or moral contradictions in much single-issue refugee advocacy. Or it fails to challenge even the most self-interested, blatantly untrue or otherwise spurious claim by any Indonesian official or commentator. These failures appear to rest on respective assumptions that the professed nobility of the cause, or polite international diplomacy, somehow gives exemption from the normal rules of informed public debate.

Third, key problems complicating implementation of the now outmoded Refugee Convention are ignored or obfuscated. Argument is particularly marred by confusion between our legal and moral responsibility to provide temporary refuge (asylum) to those genuinely needing it and our sovereign choice to target for permanent resettlement and eventual citizenship those genuine refugees who most need it. There are strong community reactions to the fact that even asylum seekers who do not qualify as refugees often now cannot be deported. Non-signatory or pseudo-signatory transit or source countries deny any responsibility to accept or protect them. By 2013 such deportations from Australia had fallen to less than 2 per cent overall and to zero with some nationalities of asylum seeker (such as Iranians). Similar problems arise with the ever-increasing number of asylum seekers who claim to be stateless, genuinely or otherwise, or who constitute a continuing national security or criminal threat despite the Convention's permitting their deportation in the former case.

Fourth, much media coverage and ensuing public argument rarely places the claims of politicians or single-issue activists in their proper context. This context particularly includes Australia's geostrategic setting, the effects of our first-world socio-economic status, the real "push" and "pull" factors consequently applying, and the way our community familiarity with mass immigration subconsciously overrides recognition that our responsibility to refugees is only to provide temporary sanctuary while needed.

In much refugee advocacy, the key difference between displaced persons and actual refugees is frequently obfuscated by lumping them in together to inflate numbers. Apples-and-oranges comparisons abound between the records of different countries in sheltering large numbers of refugees temporarily and those, such as Australia, that actually provide permanent resettlement in high per-capita and absolute numbers. That even Convention signatories have only limited obligations to those not "coming directly" from a territory where they are threatened with persecution is a point rarely conceded, as is the fact that no "right of entry" to Australia is triggered where asylum seekers have lived in, or travelled through, countries where there was no good reason why they should not have sought and obtained refuge there. Rarely mentioned is the long-term and perhaps greater moral dilemma of effectively abandoning the majority of genuine refugees to perpetual danger and misery by continually siphoning off those refugees often most equipped and needed to lead the rebuilding of their own civil societies. Other common ploys include subjective interpretations of international law and its historical background, undue reliance on the "low-numbers-currently-arriving" fallacy as a supposedly perpetual fact, and often a complete failure to consider the behaviour of neighbouring countries, particularly Indonesia.

Finally, the principle that regional solutions need to be genuinely regional in their burden-sharing – not just offer "offshore processing," "orderly arrival" and transit arrangements for eventual resettlement in Australia (or New Zealand) alone – is frequently ignored, as is the relevant and troubled 1976–96 record of the large UNHCR processing centre on Indonesia's Galang Island. This has reinforced the Indonesian belief that another major demand-pull effect would have resulted from Australia's negotiations with East Timor about establishing an offshore processing centre there (or elsewhere in the region). Moreover, while not helping genuine refugees much directly, pseudo-regional solutions counter-productively undermine the Refugee Convention and hurt the vast majority of refugees across the world. They further discourage accession and encourage further regional buck-passing and lip-service approaches to caring for refugees.

In incisive but sympathetic language, Toohey's essay avoids these pitfalls. A notable example is his analysis of Indonesia's complicity in people-smuggling through sovereign negligence, diplomatic hypocrisy, strategic apathy, official corruption, political self-interest, community empathy and severely limited policing resources. Also refreshing is his discussion of the prevalent immigration fraud and sense of entitlement among many Iranian asylum claimants in particular, and why they now form such a large proportion of claimants and rejected claims. His use of an even-handed "Occam's Razor" approach to recent events such as the burnt-hands incident and the Manus Island riots is admirable.

As opinion polls and our history consistently show, most Australians focus their compassion for refugees using three principles:

- It is impossible for Australia to shelter and particularly resettle all the world's refugees – and even all those in our region – so prioritisation and equity must be applied in practice.
- Our refugee intake, including any increases, should not occur by means outside reasonable Australian control.
- Refugees who lack the means to get to Australia and claim asylum should not be disadvantaged by those who can, especially where the former are more deserving of temporary sanctuary or permanent resettlement.

Legitimate disagreements about humanitarian priorities also arise when considering the best way to increase our capacity to offer humanitarian visas to those refugees most needing them. As do linked "ends versus means" debates, such as whether the best way to reduce in-transit drownings, or the duration and conditions of immigration detention, is to reduce unauthorised arrivals in the first place.

Effective compassion is tempered by recognition that Australia needs to exercise some degree of control over the ever-increasing numbers. This is reinforced by appreciation of the risk that the numbers could suddenly and perhaps unsustainably escalate over an unpredictable future.

Australia needs a consistent and strategically viable asylum and refugee policy, rather than one that continues to depend almost entirely on low numbers of unauthorised arrivals for its purported legitimacy, practical effectiveness, degree of community support, international acceptability and long-term operation.

Neil James

David Corlett

My first exposure to Paul Toohey's Quarterly Essay was his interview with Fran Kelly on Radio National *Breakfast*. Toohey concluded with the statement, "I certainly do agree the boats, at any cost, must be stopped." I'm not sure if this was an overstatement of his position as the seconds were counting down to the end of his interview, but as they stand, these words are remarkable. "At any cost" rules out nothing.

The government and Opposition have already indicated what they are prepared to do to stop the boats, including mandatory detention, offshore processing and, in the government's case, turning boats around. There are, however, other options that Toohey's statement opens up. Would withdrawing from the 1951 Refugee Convention be a cost worth paying? It is the Convention that binds Australia not to return refugees to situations where they may be persecuted. What about torpedoing boats on the high seas? That fits within the remit of "any cost." I'm not suggesting Toohey would advocate such things, and the latter is deliberately far-fetched (that the former is not is itself reason for concern). But his statement points to a significant question that largely goes unasked in Australian debates: what price is acceptable to stop people getting on boats coming to Australia? Or, to put it differently, what are the limits beyond which we won't go?

There is also a prior question. Why would we want to stop the boats? What is it about the boats that warrants paying such high costs to prevent them from coming? Over the years a range of answers has been given to such questions. They should be stopped because they bring to Australia people who could be terrorists. They might spread diseases. They will take our jobs. They are different from us and pose a threat to our culture and our way of life. The people on the boats don't play by the rules and are taking the places of more desperate refugees. In this sense, the boats should be stopped because those on them offend our sense of fairness (which is ironic, given the way we treat them).

More fundamentally, the boats should be stopped because they are undermining our national sovereignty: they challenge our claim that "we will decide who comes and the circumstances in which they come."

Over recent years, the reason for stopping the boats has been couched in humanitarian language. We need to stop the boats to stop the deaths. This seems obvious. Toohey writes, "If you really wanted to form an opinion on the boats, you could go to YouTube and watch the footage of the 2010 boat crashing into Christmas Island," as though there was something self-evident in this imagery, as though by seeing it you couldn't help but understand why the boats must be stopped. But this is not self-evident. Rather, Toohey's comment shows that we have come to view the arrival of boats as separate from – and, in a mixed up way, prior to – the need for protection from grave human-rights violations.

Like stories more generally, YouTube clips need to be framed. Their meanings need to be contextualised and drawn out. They need to be understood in relation to history and politics, and, most importantly, to power. The images of the boat crashing against the rocks on Christmas Island might not demonstrate to everyone who sees them *why* the boats should be stopped, as Toohey seems to imply. Raye Colbey, one of the participants in the first series of the SBS TV program *Go Back to Where You Came From*, saw that very footage and thought, "Serves you bastards right." The bastards in that distressing, terrifying clip were merely getting their just deserts – for daring to take our jobs, bludging off welfare, demanding plasma TVs, or whatever it was. I suspect Raye Colbey was not alone in holding such a view. At the political level we know from WikiLeaks that a "key Liberal Party strategist" celebrated the ongoing arrival of boats – notwithstanding the risks to their passengers – because they spelt political doom for the Labor government. The Opposition knew the human risks of ongoing boat arrivals, but rubbed its hands at the political benefits – benefits that it may have factored into its decision not to work with the Gillard government after the High Court's Malaysia Solution decision.

There is further reason to be sceptical of the humanitarian convictions of our political leaders (and sections of the media) when they continue to preside over (and barrack for) policies and practices that are not about the safety and security of those on the boats. These include sending hundreds of Sri Lankan Tamils back, after just a cursory interview, to a country still racked by grave human-rights violations, including systematic rape, torture and disappearance. Of course, there are many people on both sides of politics, as in other parts of society, who are deeply concerned by both the plight of refugees throughout the world and the loss of lives at sea to Australia's north. I don't want to suggest a sort of competition for concern, a race to the easy comfort of the moral high ground. I do want to point to the hypocrisy and short-sightedness of much of the political discourse.

Each and every death at sea is a terrible tragedy. There have been 1200 or so such tragedies since 2007. Toohey describes movingly the heartbreak of such disasters. But to those who want to use these figures as a sort of moral slam-dunk, I would say that the numbers game is a slippery one. Because at about the very time these people lost their lives, 40,000 or more people were killed – some also raped and tortured – by the Sri Lankan military. The international community largely turned a blind eye, and Australia, to suit its own political interests, continued to cosy up to the Sri Lankan government.

Of course the boats should be stopped. They should be stopped because they are unsafe, and because people are traumatised and die on them. The preferred approach of successive Australian governments has been deterrence. This involves ensuring that Australia is cruel enough, and known to be cruel enough, for asylum seekers to assess that it just doesn't make sense even to try to get here by boat. When we have been cruel enough, such as in present times, it seems to have worked.

But Australia's deterrence obsession has never addressed the key underlying reasons that people get on boats. It deals with the domestic political symptoms of the problem as perceived in Australia. And while doing so, it not only brutal-ises those people who are being used as human deterrents (including refugees), it also obscures the root causes of the irregular movement of people to Australia. For these reasons, even if it has stopped the boats, deterrence should be viewed as a policy failure. The most important cause of people getting on boats, and the one that the international refugee system was established to address, is the quest for protection from grave human-rights violations. The much-cited figure that the vast majority – around 90 per cent – of people who arrive in Australia by boat are found to be in need of international protection by Australian decision-makers is evidence that protection from persecution and other serious human-rights violations remains central to this political and policy area. This, the protection of refugees from persecution, and not "stopping the boats," is the measure of policy success.

Of course, people get on boats for reasons other than protection from per-secution, and Toohey's essay offers some important insights into this. It does so with admirable sensitivity, neither demonising nor romanticising those who would make that journey. In laying bare the humanity of those involved, Toohey points to some of the complexity confronting policy-makers. For example, where do those who are merely "rolling the dice, having a go" fit into a system whose raison d'être is to offer protection for those with no choice but to seek it outside their homelands?

Toohey's treatment of the Iranians he meets highlights this issue. Many Persian Iranians, he suggests, do not meet the definition of a refugee. This is not to say that life for them in Iran is good; he writes that they "saw themselves living a bellowing daily tragedy under the totalitarian mullahs. If life was passably survivable, it did not follow that it was acceptable or tolerable." They wanted freedom and they wanted opportunity. These are noble aspirations (and one of the many curious things about Australian political discourse is that such ambitions have become something worthy of disparaging if you seek to arrive in Australia by boat). But they do not qualify you to be a refugee. Somewhere, lines must be drawn. A sad story, even a story of utter desperation, is not enough. What do we do with people whom Australia does not owe an obligation to protect? They should be expected to return. But what if they don't want to return? The Australian government is within its rights to compel them to do so. But what if, like Iran, the states from which they have come do not accept forced returns? Australia is in a bind.

The choice that Australia has continued to make is not only to brutalise people to stop them from getting on boats, but also, when they will not return, to humiliate and belittle them, to destroy them psychologically within the detention system across Australia and the Pacific. We have detained asylum seekers until they cannot take it any longer, until they feel compelled either to return or to risk insanity. Australia and the organisation it pays to do the dirty work of returning such people, the International Organisation for Migration, call this "voluntary" return. It is not. One of the problems with Australia's slow psychological destruction of asylum seekers in detention is that many have agreed to return "voluntarily" to situations in which they have indeed been persecuted. Some have been killed.

Australia's approach consistently is that of a one-trick pony. We just need to be tougher. If the boats keep coming, get tougher still. We seem uninterested in being smarter. In February, Reza Barati was killed on Manus Island. From reports in the media, it is unlikely he was a refugee. He was an architect seeking a better life. If he had known that he would be brutalised in Australia's offshore detention system and then beaten to death, he is unlikely to have chosen to take a boat. The cost wouldn't have been worth the benefit. But I wonder if other factors – other than the most cruel and, indeed, deadly – could have affected his decision. While Australia has a migration program that allows for skilled and family migration, this is highly competitive – tens of thousands of applications are rejected annually, and presumably many other people do not even bother applying because they know that they would not be able to meet the visa requirements. Would Reza Barati have chanced it on a boat if there were realistic alternative migration routes to his dream of a better life?

What if Australia took an even bigger-picture perspective? The Iranian economy is crippled by sanctions imposed by the US and the UN Security Council. The recently elected "reformist" president has indicated a willingness to engage with the international community, including being prepared to limit the extent to which Iran enriches uranium and to open its nuclear program to international inspectors in exchange for lifting the sanctions. Would a more vibrant Iranian economy, the opportunity for prosperity surrounded by friends and family, have been incentive enough to stop Reza Barati and those like him from making that fateful boat journey? And what would a more open economy mean for political and religious freedom in Iran? Would the prospect of greater freedom give hope to the many millions of Iranians who, while not refugees, continue to yearn for genuine liberty?

While Toohey writes compellingly of the missed opportunities to engage Indonesia on asylum seekers, his Indonesian Solution would not address these issues. The "solution," to the extent that the problem of displacement and irregular migration can be "solved" at all, must be multifaceted, multilateral and evidence-based. While it would be possible to overstate our influence, Australia is a middle power that is both a close ally of the US and a current seat-holder on the UN Security Council. We could use this position to seek to improve the lives of Iranians, Sri Lankans, Afghans and others who might otherwise get on boats – both in their countries of origin and in third countries. Of course, Indonesia would also be key. Furthermore, as well as political influence, Australia has indicated that it has significant resources to put towards these issues if it so chooses. The government has allocated about $4 billion in 2013–14 to stop the boats. This is roughly the same amount of money that the UN High Commissioner for Refugees spends to protect nearly 40 million displaced people across the globe. Now that the boats appear to have stopped, there are real opportunities, if we are serious, to respond to the reasons why people have sought to get to Australia by boat, including building the capacity in our region to protect the persecuted. If we are prepared to stop the boats "at any cost," what are we prepared to pay to protect the persecuted?

David Corlett

Correspondence

Andrew Hamilton

The great gift Paul Toohey brings to the readers of his essay is his assiduousness as a journalist. He complements the broad and abstract simplicities of the asylum-seeker debate by depicting the complex human reality of people who claim asylum and of those with whom they interact in order to make their claim. He introduces the reader to not one but three groups of Iranian asylum seekers, describes the local face of people smuggling and speaks with officials at the US–Mexico border to see how they respond to human traffic across borders. He shows the variety of human motives and responses of asylum seekers and others, ranging from stoicism to exploitation, to greed, to unselfishness and to attempting to live ordinary human lives in extraordinary circumstances.

The complexity of this reality challenges simple views. As a strong critic of Australian policy, I found Toohey's description of the human devastation caused by travelling in overcrowded and unseaworthy boats particularly confronting. I was familiar from many personal stories with the huge loss of life among Cambodians smuggled across the minefields at the Thai border and among Vietnamese at the hands of pirates or from storms off the Thai coast. But Toohey's account of those who were lost and who survived from one boat brings out the horror and grief for each person affected. It was part of the risk. But should it have been?

Toohey also asks why Australia did not seriously engage with Indonesia in order to find a regional solution for people who sought protection. It is clear from the account that Australia did not engage with anyone for a regional solution. Its sole goal was to stop people arriving in Australia by boat to make a claim for protection. The botched East Timor solution, the addled Malaysia Solution, the brutal Pacific Solution and the pushing back of boats have not been about building partnerships. They have been about using our neighbours. It makes one fear for the time when Australia needs regional goodwill.

The essay is a tribute to the journalist's craft. Toohey travels rough, keeps on asking questions, allows everyone their story without accepting their veracity. His great enemy is bullshit of any kind. But his essay also hints at the personal cost of being there as an observer and reporter of the human mess. His humanity is patent when engaging with the survivors of shipwreck who have lost their children, and in his judgments of politicians who have lost sight of the pain of ordinary people.

Toohey's careful focus on the messy human reality known as "the asylum-seeker problem" naturally raises larger questions that lie outside his remit. It leads us to ask how we ought, as citizens and as a nation, respond to the people who claim our protection on more or less compelling grounds, to the people who encourage them to come and who bring them, and to the people and nations they pass through on the way. What moral compass ought to guide Australian policy? And what are the consequences for Australian culture and society if we act badly?

The heart of ethics is to treat people with respect for their humanity. In Toohey's account, some asylum seekers make a compelling case for protection by Australia by reason of the persecution they face in their own country. Respect demands that we meet their claim. The claim of others for protection is not compelling. So there is a need to hear and adjudicate the claims of all. Blanket or arbitrary dismissal of claims without adjudication is lacking in due respect, whether it happens by summary repatriation or by pushing back boats.

Due respect for people is also inconsistent with using them as means to our ends. Australian refugee policy has long used prolonged detention as a means of deterring others from coming by boat to claim asylum. The harsh conditions of detention on Manus Island and Nauru, with their inevitable consequences of mental illness and violence, with no possibility of settling in Australia, are an even more brutal example of bad means being used to achieve bad ends.

Respect also means working cooperatively to share the burden of supporting people who seek asylum, penalising those who exploit them, and obviating the need to risk life travelling on unsafe boats. This demands regional negotiations that look to the good of all and not simply to preventing people from making claims on Australia.

Many dismiss any call for an ethical compass in asylum-seeker policy-making as unrealistic moralising or grandstanding. Certainly in the present climate the call is not heard. But the advantage of an ethical compass is that, even if you choose to ignore it, you are better able to anticipate the harmful consequences for yourself of doing so. In asylum-seeker policy they are evident both in Australia's relationships with its neighbours and in its own society.

The lack of respect for people who seek protection from Australia is echoed in the lack of respect for our neighbours. They are means to be used, accommodated, bullied, ignored, paid off or duchessed in the pursuit of excluding asylum seekers. Certainly, some have their price, but using them to traffic human beings usually creates resentment and contempt. It is not conducive to cooperation in the things we take to be more important, like non-human trade.

Any lack of respect by governments for people who seek protection will also naturally be extended to others in the community. If it is seen as fair to return people to unknown danger without a hearing, to treat them badly in order to send signals to others, and to remove them from the protection of the rule of law, it will also be readily assumed that others can be treated in the same way: indigenous Australians, the unemployed, Muslims, take your pick. The membrane of respect, mutual trust and responsibility that protects a just society from the bacteria of tyranny is fragile. The cost of Australia's treatment of people who seek protection has yet to be counted and paid.

Andrew Hamilton

Paul Toohey

My intention with *That Sinking Feeling* was to take a working journalist's approach to the asylum subject. That meant reporting what I saw, reflecting how we in the news business react to hastily unfurled policy, and relating its immediate effects. I had no desire to write an explosive polemic. That is probably a poor approach to business, but my view is that if neither the Left nor the Right liked it, then I may have succeeded.

If I had my time again, I would go deeper into how an Indonesian Solution might work. That said, I don't see it as my role to propose policy; nor did it follow from the essay's subtitle, "The Search for the Indonesian Solution," that I held one up my sleeve.

Furthermore, with the spying revelations, along with the lifeboats and the push-backs, which caused a substantial slowdown in boat traffic but also a freezing in relations, the chance for an Indonesian Solution had passed at the time the essay was published. It remains passed.

Yet an answer *was* in front of our eyes the whole time. It lay on the island of Java.

Java, the most populous of the Indonesian islands, was already serving as Australia's de facto offshore facility for asylum seekers. After Kevin Rudd ordered the closure of Manus and Nauru in late 2007, there was never any need for Australia to reopen offshore detention centres. There was one; it was just never described as such.

Java is – or, until this particular asylum-seeking cycle was more or less broken by Rudd and then Tony Abbott, was – the holding pen. People gathered in the west Javan city of Cisarua. There were no guards and no walls. But the people trying to get to Australia were hardly invisible. They were a known and quantifiable presence.

The problem was they were taking boats, in large numbers, to Australia.

President Susilo Bambang Yudhoyono sympathised with Australia's political problem, but was concerned not to give himself domestic political grief by focusing too heavily on asylum seekers. Indonesia's political elite always considered them an Australian problem, because that's where they were headed.

A shrewd approach would have been for Australia to see the problem from SBY's point of view, rather than its own. That could have seen a three-point proposition that sought to stem the flow of asylum seekers making landfall in Indonesia in the first place.

Significant reductions in people arriving in Indonesia could have been achieved, firstly, by taking a more critical look at those coming by plane. Indonesia began doing this in July last year, by ending visas-on-arrival for Iranians. The policy could have extended to other nations and ethnicities using the asylum trail. It would have required Australian funding to improve professionalism at Indonesian airports.

This could have worked together with a second strand that saw Indonesia making more active interventions off the southern coast of Java. Indonesia fundamentally lacks the ability to control inward and outward movement from its coasts because it does not have the boats. Properly equipped with two or three fully fledged, Australian-gifted naval vessels, concentrated at the known departure points, Indonesia could have provided a much stronger gauntlet that let asylum seekers know there was no easy run down to Christmas Island.

The third approach would have been to give Indonesia arms-length assistance to better police the waters in the short hop from Malaysia, which is how most asylum seekers arrive in Indonesia while trying to get to Australia. This is the decision that would have taken most Australian courage, because Malaysia would not have liked it. But Malaysia does not particularly like us, or Indonesia, anyway; and, as I hope I made clear in the essay, investing in Indonesia is a far better short- and long-term strategy than playing games with erratic Malaysia.

A sea blockade of sorts would have forced Malaysia to reconsider its own absurdly gregarious open-visa policy for all comers, the main cause of the asylum problem as far as Australia and Indonesia are concerned.

Preventing unknowns from arriving unannounced is every country's right. People departing Malaysia on fast boats through the Malacca or Singapore straits breach Indonesia's sovereignty every night. Taking defensive action would have been a legitimate Indonesian undertaking.

This would have required that Indonesia create its own stop-the-boats policy – an interesting thought. But Australians, I believe, misunderstand Indonesia's position: it appreciates Abbott's sovereignty argument. What it does not enjoy is Australia acting without consultation.

There would also have been a small reverse cost to Indonesia for stopping the Malaysian incursions: it would have needed to end its own nightly outbound human shipments on the maid trade, as Indonesian domestics head to staff the homes of the Malaysian and Singaporean elite for pitiful wages. But this is a problem that urgently needs to be addressed.

Malaysia has been the unspoken problem in the asylum chain. It is the regional asylum and refugee bottleneck. It, not Australia or Indonesia, is home to the real crisis. Malaysia has permitted an airport arrival-visa free-for-all, and it has secretly welcomed the under-the-radar Indonesian workers who work in near-slave conditions. Despite the Malaysian leaders' Etonian tones, they're the rednecks of Asia.

Would these measures have cost Australia more than Nauru, Manus or the money already allegedly paid to Malaysia for a solution that never took off? I'm not sure; but none of them would have trespassed on Indonesian sovereignty. They would have strengthened it. And it would have been a timely statement on whom Australia valued most in the region.

A good friend, as we claim to be, does not act unilaterally to send boats back. And Indonesia has been a poor friend in allowing so many boats to come our way. But what it needed, though was too proud to ask, was our assistance.

Abbott's promise to make Jakarta his foreign-relations priority has disappeared. He needs to win back this crucial partner, which in early May became, according to the World Bank, the world's tenth-largest economy, and will within several decades become the fifth-largest. We are going to need them more than they need us.

I take no issue with any of the correspondents' comments on That Sinking Feeling and acknowledge a rare achievement in this particular debate: that those who took issue did so without hostility.

Paul Toohey
Darwin, May 2014

Michael Bachelard is Fairfax Media's Indonesia correspondent. A former political reporter and workplace relations writer, he was awarded a Jefferson Fellowship in journalism in 2005. He is the author of *Behind the Exclusive Brethren*.

Andrew Charlton is the author of *Ozonomics, Fair Trade for All* (with Joseph Stiglitz) and Quarterly Essay 44, *Man-Made World*, which won the 2012 John Button Prize. From 2008 to 2010 he was senior economic adviser to Prime Minister Kevin Rudd. He has worked at the London School of Economics, the United Nations and Boston Consulting Group and studied at Oxford University as a Rhodes Scholar.

David Corlett is a writer and adjunct research fellow at the Swinburne Institute for Social Research. He has worked with refugees and asylum seekers as a case worker, researcher and adviser, and is the author of *Following Them Home* and *Stormy Weather*. He was the presenter of SBS TV's *Go Back To Where You Came From*.

Mary Crock is professor of public law at the University of Sydney. She has worked with refugees and asylum seekers since 1989, when she helped establish Melbourne's first community legal centre specialising in immigration and refugee law.

Andrew Hamilton is editorial consultant at Jesuit Communications and contributes regularly to *Eureka Street*. He has written widely on refugee issues, and has been Catholic chaplain at an Immigration Detention Centre for many years.

Neil James has been executive director of the Australia Defence Association since early 2003. His previous thirty-one years of military service included working at the United Nations headquarters in New York, with multinational peacekeeping and humanitarian operations in the field, and as head of the joint intelligence branch at Headquarters Northern Command in Darwin.

Paul Toohey is chief northern correspondent for the *Australian*. He won a Walkley Award for his first Quarterly Essay, *Last Drinks: The Impact of the Northern Territory Intervention*. He was previously a senior writer at the *Bulletin* and is the author of three books: *God's Little Acre, Rocky Goes West* and *The Killer Within*. He has won the Graham Perkin journalist of the year award and a Walkley award for magazine feature writing. He lives in Darwin.

SUBSCRIBE to Quarterly Essay & SAVE over 25% on the cover price

Subscriptions: Receive a discount and never miss an issue. Mailed direct to your door.
- ☐ **1 year subscription** (4 issues): $59 within Australia incl. GST. Outside Australia $89.
- ☐ **2 year subscription** (8 issues): $105 within Australia incl. GST. Outside Australia $165.
* All prices include postage and handling.

Back Issues: (Prices include postage and handling.)

- ☐ **QE 2** ($15.99) John Birmingham *Appeasing Jakarta*
- ☐ **QE 4** ($15.99) Don Watson *Rabbit Syndrome*
- ☐ **QE 6** ($15.99) John Button *Beyond Belief*
- ☐ **QE 7** ($15.99) John Martinkus *Paradise Betrayed*
- ☐ **QE 8** ($15.99) Amanda Lohrey *Groundswell*
- ☐ **QE 10** ($15.99) Gideon Haigh *Bad Company*
- ☐ **QE 11** ($15.99) Germaine Greer *Whitefella Jump Up*
- ☐ **QE 12** ($15.99) David Malouf *Made in England*
- ☐ **QE 13** ($15.99) Robert Manne with David Corlett *Sending Them Home*
- ☐ **QE 14** ($15.99) Paul McGeough *Mission Impossible*
- ☐ **QE 15** ($15.99) Margaret Simons *Latham's World*
- ☐ **QE 17** ($15.99) John Hirst *"Kangaroo Court"*
- ☐ **QE 18** ($15.99) Gail Bell *The Worried Well*
- ☐ **QE 19** ($15.99) Judith Brett *Relaxed & Comfortable*
- ☐ **QE 20** ($15.99) John Birmingham *A Time for War*
- ☐ **QE 21** ($15.99) Clive Hamilton *What's Left?*
- ☐ **QE 22** ($15.99) Amanda Lohrey *Voting for Jesus*
- ☐ **QE 23** ($15.99) Inga Clendinnen *The History Question*
- ☐ **QE 24** ($15.99) Robyn Davidson *No Fixed Address*
- ☐ **QE 25** ($15.99) Peter Hartcher *Bipolar Nation*
- ☐ **QE 26** ($15.99) David Marr *His Master's Voice*
- ☐ **QE 27** ($15.99) Ian Lowe *Reaction Time*
- ☐ **QE 28** ($15.99) Judith Brett *Exit Right*
- ☐ **QE 29** ($15.99) Anne Manne *Love & Money*
- ☐ **QE 30** ($15.99) Paul Toohey *Last Drinks*
- ☐ **QE 31** ($15.99) Tim Flannery *Now or Never*
- ☐ **QE 32** ($15.99) Kate Jennings *American Revolution*
- ☐ **QE 33** ($15.99) Guy Pearse *Quarry Vision*
- ☐ **QE 34** ($15.99) Annabel Crabb *Stop at Nothing*
- ☐ **QE 36** ($15.99) Mungo MacCallum *Australian Story*
- ☐ **QE 37** ($15.99) Waleed Aly *What's Right?*
- ☐ **QE 38** ($15.99) David Marr *Power Trip*
- ☐ **QE 39** ($15.99) Hugh White *Power Shift*
- ☐ **QE 42** ($15.99) Judith Brett *Fair Share*
- ☐ **QE 43** ($15.99) Robert Manne *Bad News*
- ☐ **QE 44** ($15.99) Andrew Charlton *Man-Made World*
- ☐ **QE 45** ($15.99) Anna Krien *Us and Them*
- ☐ **QE 46** ($15.99) Laura Tingle *Great Expectations*
- ☐ **QE 47** ($15.99) David Marr *Political Animal*
- ☐ **QE 48** ($15.99) Tim Flannery *After the Future*
- ☐ **QE 49** ($15.99) Mark Latham *Not Dead Yet*
- ☐ **QE 50** ($15.99) Anna Goldsworthy *Unfinished Business*
- ☐ **QE 51** ($15.99) David Marr *The Prince*
- ☐ **QE 52** ($15.99) Linda Jaivin *Found in Translation*
- ☐ **QE 53** ($15.99) Paul Toohey *That Sinking Feeling*

Payment Details: I enclose a cheque/money order made out to Schwartz Publishing Pty Ltd. Please debit my credit card (Mastercard or Visa accepted).

Card No. ☐☐☐☐ ☐☐☐☐ ☐☐☐☐ ☐☐☐☐

Expiry date / **CCV** **Amount $**

Cardholder's name **Signature**

Name

Address

Email **Phone**

Post or fax this form to: Quarterly Essay, Reply Paid 79448, Collingwood VIC 3066 /
Tel: (03) 9486 0288 / Fax: (03) 9486 0244 / Email: subscribe@blackincbooks.com
Subscribe online at **www.quarterlyessay.com**